ADULTPIANO Adventures® CLASSICS

Symphony Themes, Opera Gems and Classical Favorites **1**

Arranged by Nancy and Randall Faber

Production Coordinator: Jon Ophoff
Cover: Terpstra Design, San Francisco
Engraving: Dovetree Productions, Inc.

FABER
PIANO ADVENTURES®

ISBN 978-1-61677-186-7

OREWORD

A "classic" is a work of art or literature that is recognized to be of the highest quality. Many works of art were popular in their day, but later forgotten. A classic, however, withstands the test of time—it endures to be appreciated and enjoyed by later generations.

Adult Piano Adventures® Classics Book 1 celebrates great masterworks of Western Music. This book is designed for adult beginners and for those who have played piano in the past and are reacquainting with the keyboard. Those exploring the piano for the first time will find the arrangements appealing and well within reach. Adults returning to the keyboard can "brush up on basics" while exploring important orchestral and operatic works.

This book has three sections.

- Section 1 features piano arrangements with minimal hand position changes. Many selections include an optional duet part.

- Section 2 introduces the I, IV, and V7 chords in the key of C major. With these three chords, a pianist can play many classical melodies.

- Section 3 presents the I, IV, and V7 chords in the key of G major, with arrangements of Vivaldi's *Autumn* (from *The Four Seasons*), Mozart's theme from *The Magic Flute*, and Lizst's *Liebestraum*.

Enjoy! And may the melodies of Bach, Beethoven, Brahms, and other master composers bring you meaningful musical memories.

TABLE OF CONTENTS

BEGINNING CLASSICS

The first section offers introductory arrangements
with simple harmonies.

THEME FROM SYMPHONY NO. 104 (London Symphony) - page 6

Haydn is rightly called "the father of the modern symphony" – he wrote 108 of
them! Toward the end of his life, Haydn was twice invited to London. For these
trips (each of them lasting well over a year), he wrote 12 works that we now call
the "London Symphonies." This is the main theme from the last of these
symphonies, No. 104, written in 1795.

SWAN LAKE (Overture to Act II) - page 7

Tchaikovsky was the greatest Russian composer of the 19th century. His music
is melodious, dramatic, and imbued with a strong nationalistic flavor. *Swan Lake*
was the first of Tchaikovsky's three ballets. At the opening of Act II, the Swan
Maidens dance on the banks of a moonlit lake. Prince Siegfried encounters the
Swan Queen and discovers that she is Princess Odette, changed into a swan by
an evil sorcerer.

ODE TO JOY (Theme from the Ninth Symphony) - page 8

This melody is from Beethoven's last symphony. Beethoven included a chorus
(something new at the time), and this melody is sung in the final movement. The
words by the great German poet Friedrich Schiller celebrate the brotherhood of
man. This music is often called the "Ode to Joy" because the text highlights the
word *freude* – joy. Both the music and words are majestic and spiritual.

ALLELUIA (from *Exultate Jubilate*) - page 10

This is the main theme from the third movement of a motet entitled Exultate
Jubilate. Mozart wrote this brilliant concerto for voice and orchestra for Venanzio
Rauzzini, a famous castrato (male soprano) of the time. Rauzzini premiered the
motet in Milan in 1773. This motet and the Requiem are Mozart's best-known
sacred compositions.

POMP AND CIRCUMSTANCE (Op. 39, No. 1) - page 12

Sir Edward Elgar wrote five Pomp and Circumstance marches, but it is the first
march, written in 1901, that everyone knows. To Americans, this solemn and
majestic melody is associated with high school graduations. To the British, it is
almost regarded as a national anthem. With words by Arthur Christopher Benson,
it has become known as Land of Hope and Glory.

FINALE (from Symphony No. 1) - page 14

Brahms began writing his symphony at age 22. He worked on the first movement
for several years, but put it aside. It took him 21 years to complete the symphony!
Even just before its premier in 1876, he made cuts in some movements. The
symphony is in the key of C minor, but a change to the major key in the Finale
signals the triumph of glory over struggle.

AIR (from the Anna Magdalena Bach Notebook) - page 16

Johann Sebastian Bach presented his second wife, Anna Magdalena, with two notebooks (1722 and 1725) of short, easy keyboard pieces. Some pieces in the collection were composed by Bach himself, others by Bach family friends. The graceful melody in this book is from the 1725 collection. In Leipzig, teaching was part of Bach's job, and he used these collections as teaching pieces. Music from these notebooks is still played by all serious music students.

AUTUMN, first movement (from *The Four Seasons*) - page 18

Vivaldi, a native Venetian, was known as "il Prete Rosso" (the priest with red hair). In 1703 he became the violin teacher at the Pio Ospedale della Pietà, an institution that cared for orphaned and indigent girls. Those who showed talent were given musical training. A good number of Vivaldi's works, like the "Four Seasons" concerto, were composed for this female orchestra.

FINALE (from Symphony No. 9, *From the New World*) - page 20

Dvořák spent three years (1892-95) in the United States. This symphony was the first work he completed there, and it was meant to serve as an example of his theory that "American music" could be made from Indian and Negro themes. He said, "Everyone who has a nose must smell America in this symphony." None of the music, however, directly quotes any folk melodies.

HORNPIPE (from *Water Music*) - page 22

When King George I took a barge ride on the Thames with his court, Handel accompanied the royal boat on another barge, complete with orchestra. Water Music is divided into three suites. This piece from the second suite is a hornpipe – a sailor's dance. In it, Handel makes special use of the brass instruments. The trumpets and horns echo each other in antiphonal sound effects.

HUNTSMEN'S CHORUS (from *Der Freischütz*) - page 24

This chorus is sung in the third act of Carl Maria von Weber's best-known opera, *Der Freischütz* (The Sharpshooter). It was wildly successful at the time (premiered in 1821) chiefly because it combined exotic and Germanic folk-like elements. Complete with fiends, forests, magic bullets, and exciting orchestral effects, this opera became the model for Romantic operas (which often featured demonic characters), including the mammoth works of Richard Wagner.

THEME FROM BEETHOVEN'S FIFTH SYMPHONY - page 26

The four-note opening of Beethoven's Fifth Symphony may be the most famous musical theme in the world. The theme is woven into almost every bar of the opening movement, and the music is full of dramatic contrasts and abrupt changes of tempo and texture. Even if you imagine "fate knocking at the door," there is no doubt that human nature triumphs by the end of the symphony.

Theme from
Symphony No. 104
("London" Symphony)

Franz Joseph Haydn
(1732-1809)

Teacher Duet: (Student plays 1 octave higher the first time, and 2 octaves higher on repeat)

Swan Lake

(Overture to Act II)

Peter Ilyich Tchaikovsky
(1840-1893)

Moderato

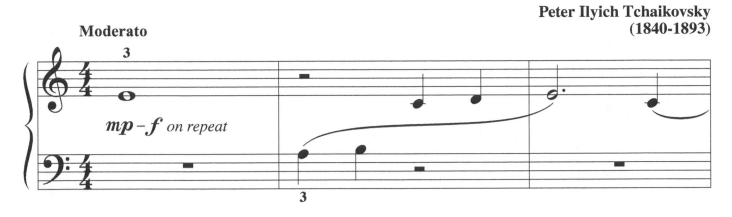

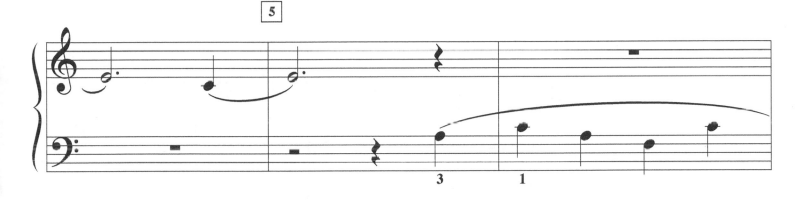

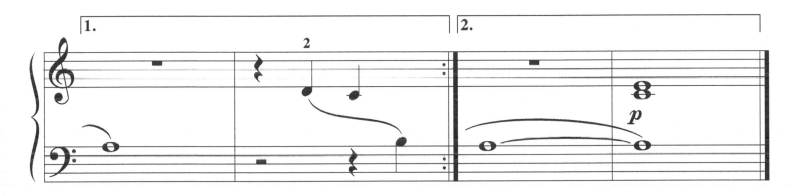

Teacher Duet: (Student plays 1 octave higher)

FF3030

8

Ode to Joy
(Theme from the Ninth Symphony)

Ludwig van Beethoven
(1770-1827)

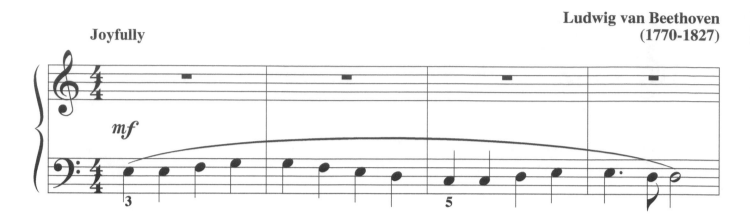

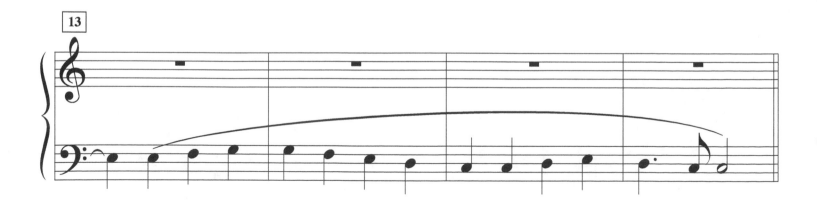

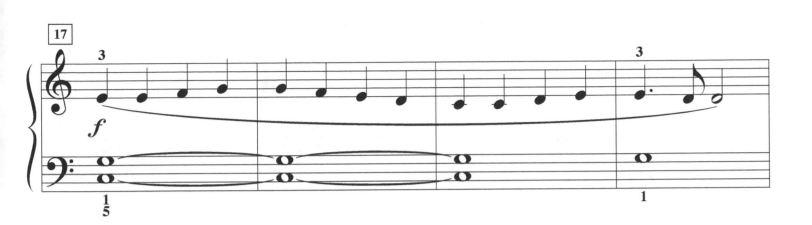

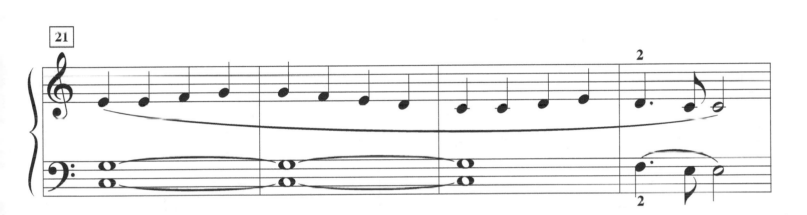

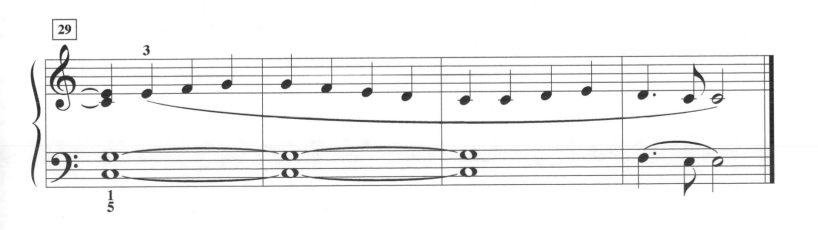

Alleluia
(from *Exultate Jubilate*)

Wolfgang Amadeus Mozart
(1756-1791)

Allegro

f Al - le - lu - ia, Al - le - lu - ia, _____

5

Al - le - lu - ia, Al - le - lu - ia.

Teacher Duet: (Student plays 1 octave higher)

R.H.

L.H. *mp*
with pedal

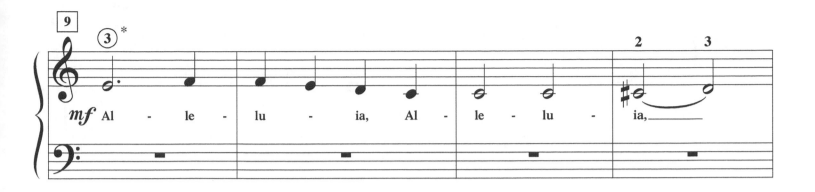

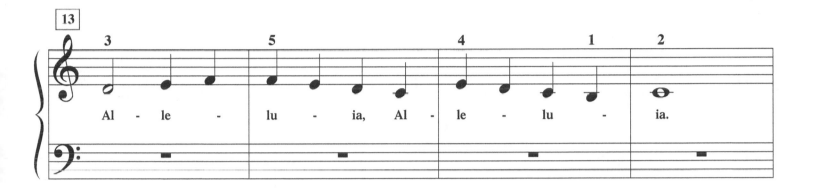

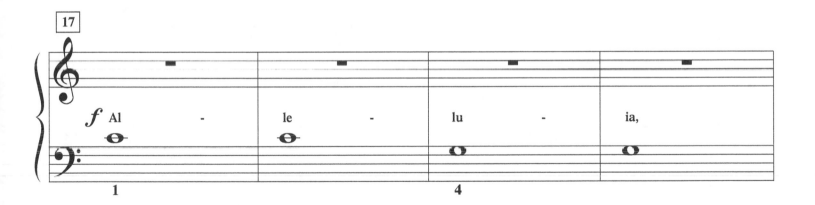

* A circled finger number indicates a hand position change on the keyboard.

Pomp and Circumstance

(Op. 39, No. 1 - Trio)

Sir Edward Elgar
(1857-1934)

Allegro moderato

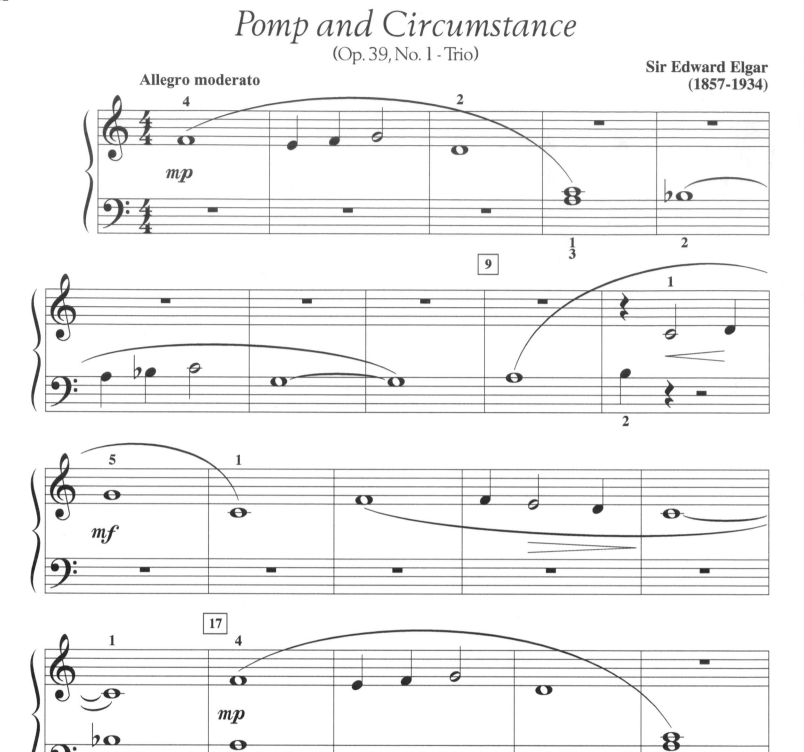

Teacher Duet: (Student plays 1 octave higher)

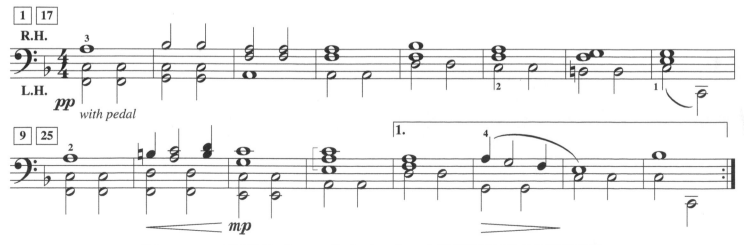

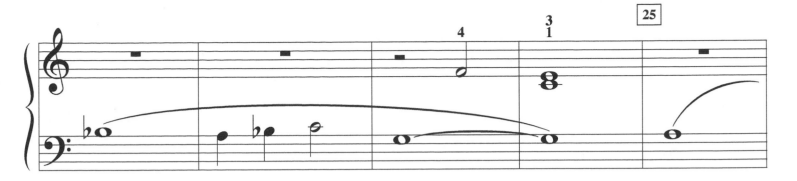

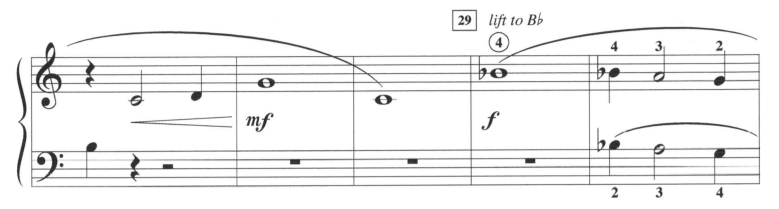

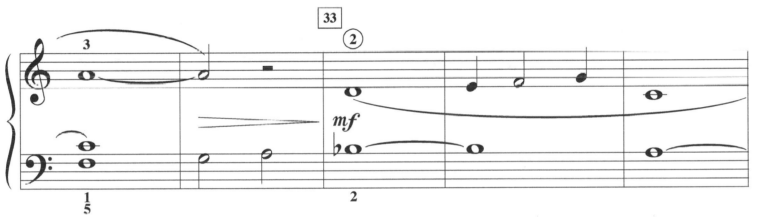

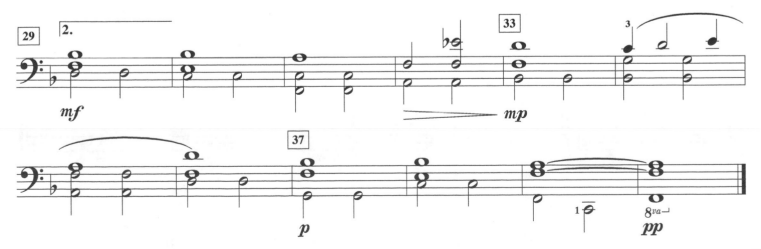

Finale

(from Symphony No. 1)

Johannes Brahms
(1833-1897)

Not too fast, but spirited

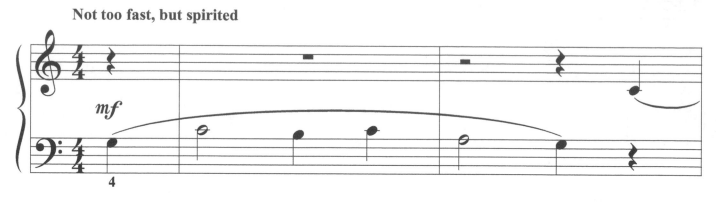

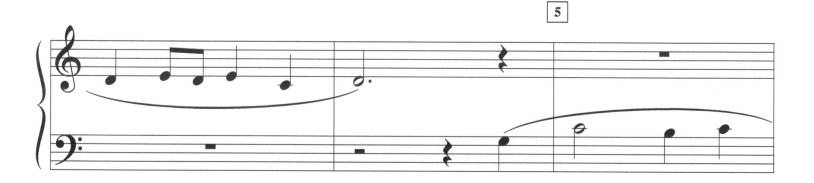

Teacher Duet: (Student plays 1 octave higher)

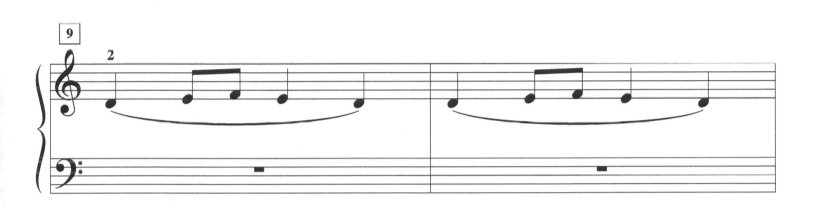

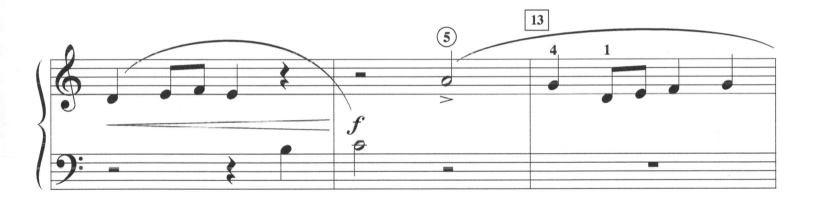

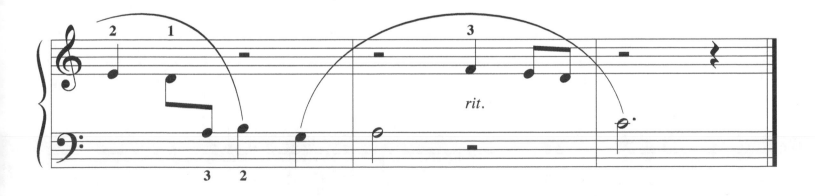

Air
(from the Anna Magdalena Bach Notebook)

Johann Sebastian Bach
(1685-1750)

Moderato

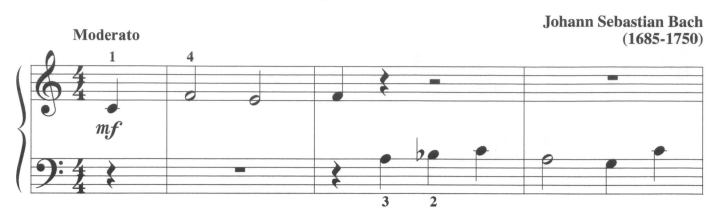

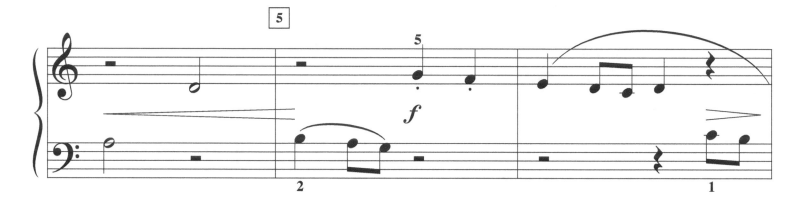

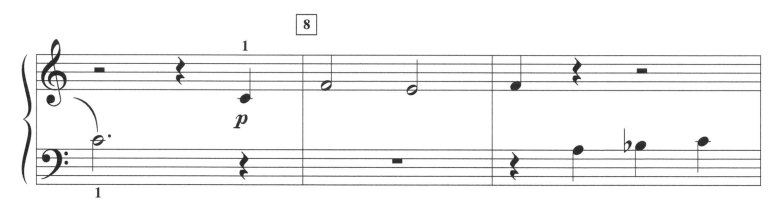

Teacher Duet: (Student plays 1 octave higher)

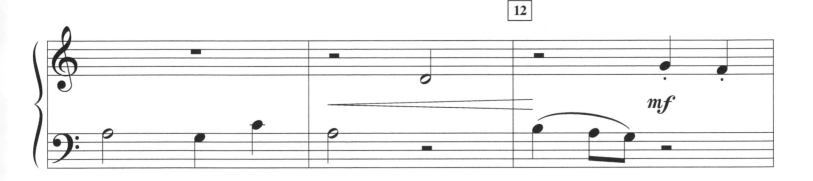

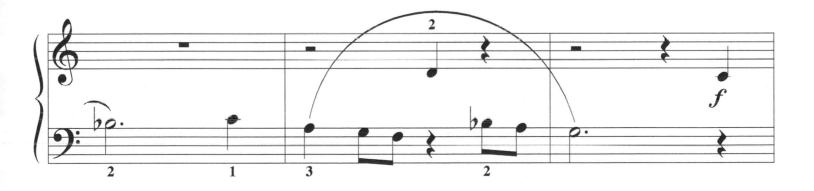

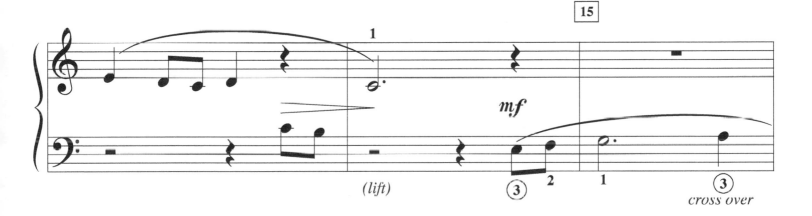

Autumn, 1st movement

(from *The Four Seasons*)

Antonio Vivaldi
(1678-1741)

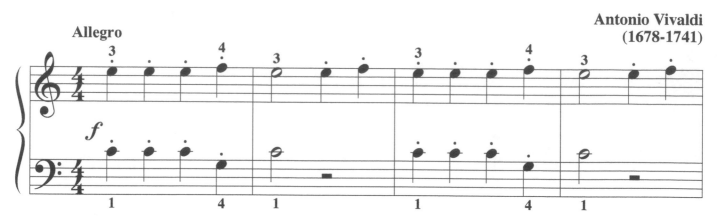

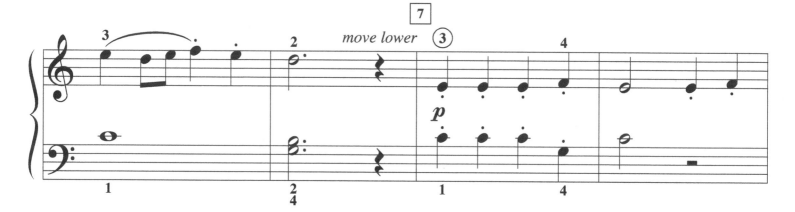

Teacher Duet: (Student plays 1 octave higher)

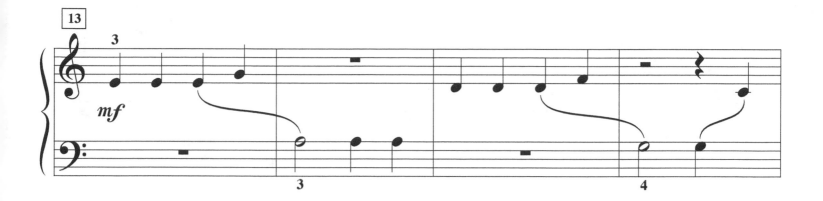

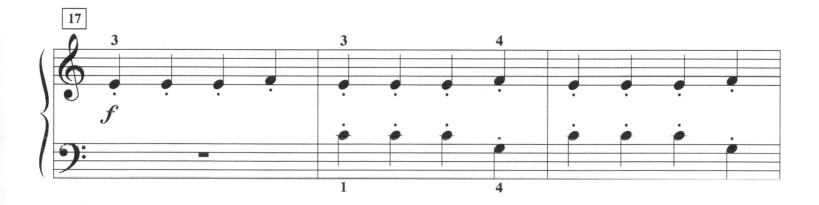

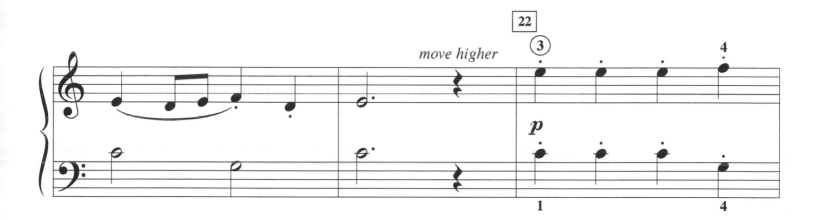

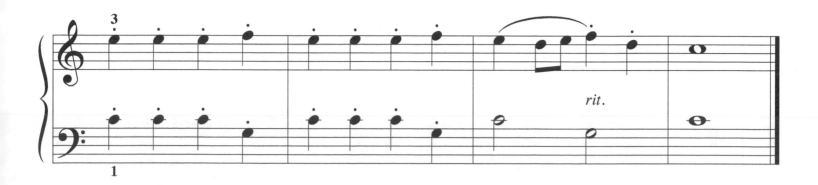

Finale

(from Symphony No. 9, *From the New World*)

Antonín Dvořák
(1841-1904)

Strong and vigorous

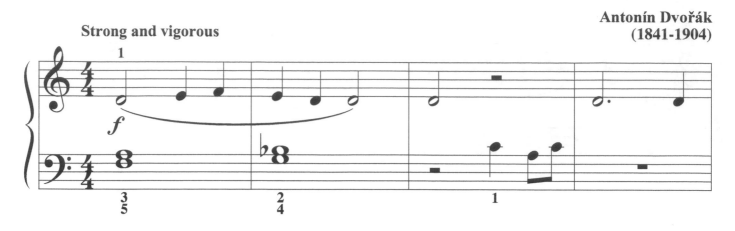

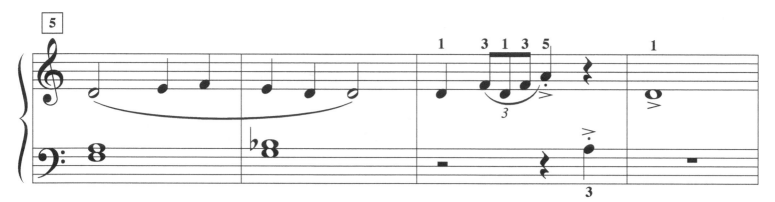

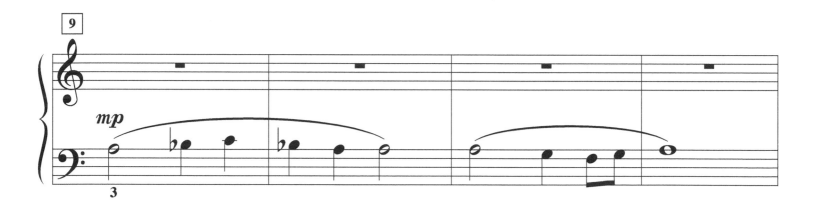

Teacher Duet: (Student plays 1 octave higher)

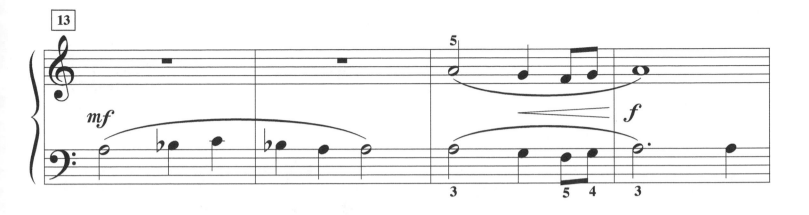

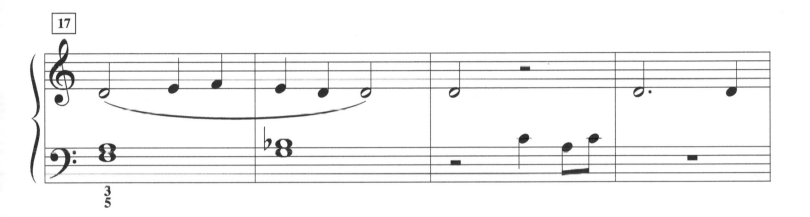

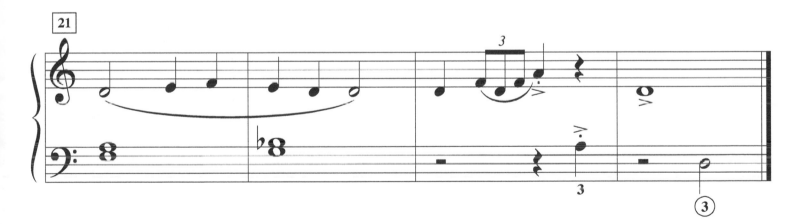

Hornpipe
(from *Water Music*)

George Frideric Handel
(1685-1759)

Teacher Duet: (Student plays 1 octave higher)

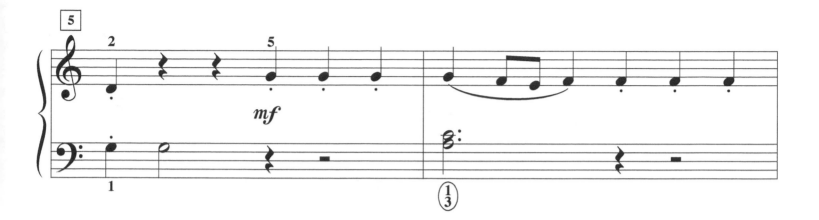

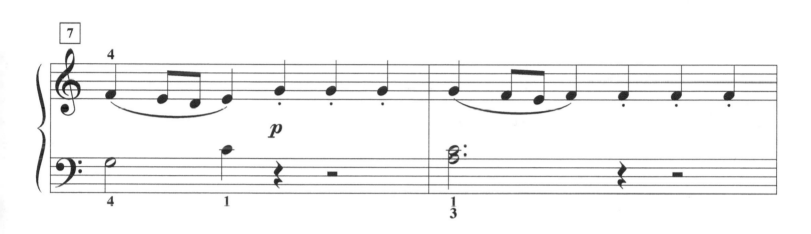

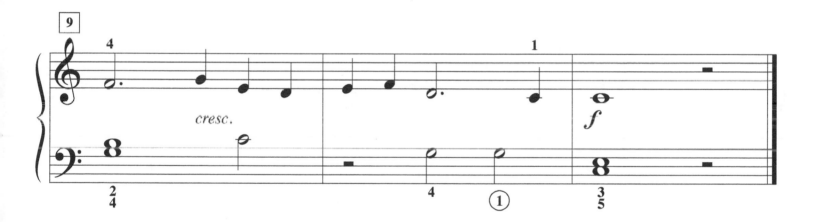

Huntsmen's Chorus
(from *Der Freischütz*)

Carl Maria von Weber
(1786-1826)

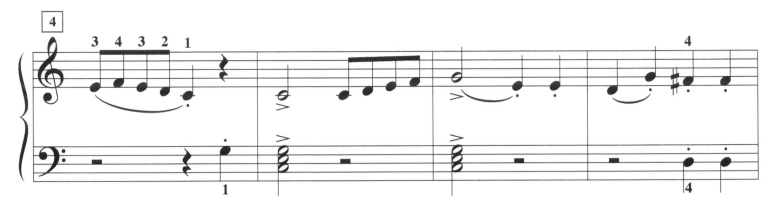

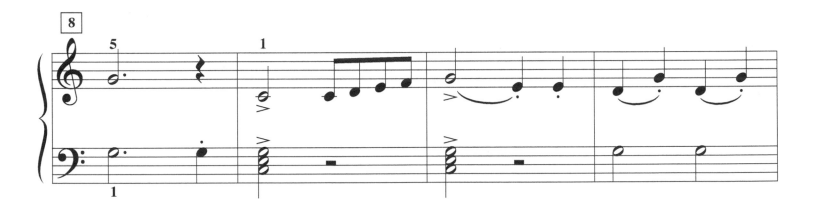

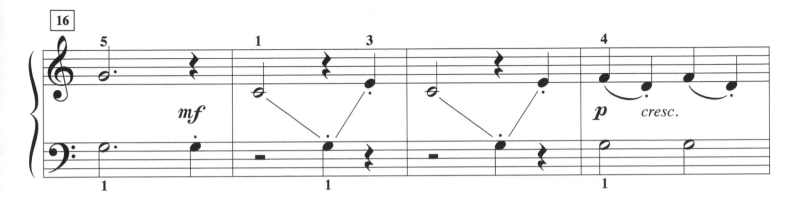

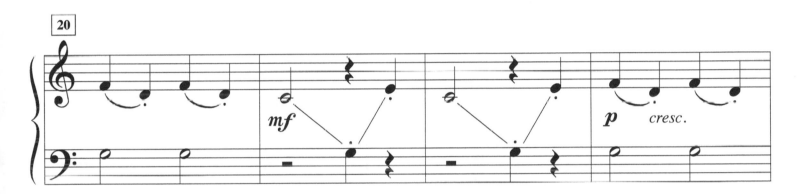

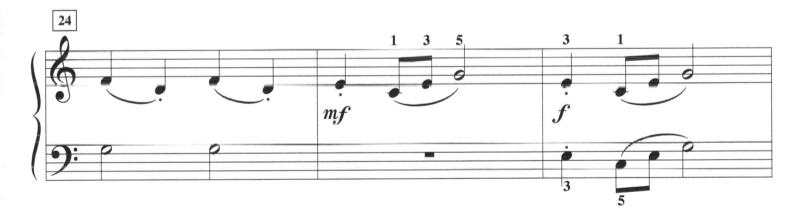

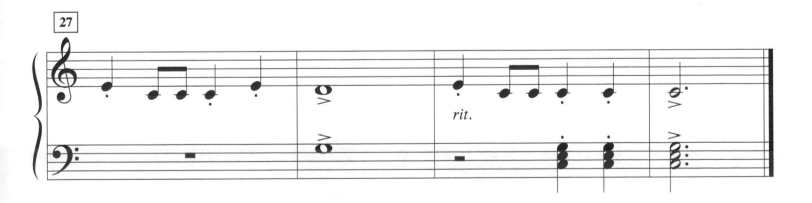

Theme from
Beethoven's
Fifth Symphony

Ludwig van Beethoven
(1770-1827)

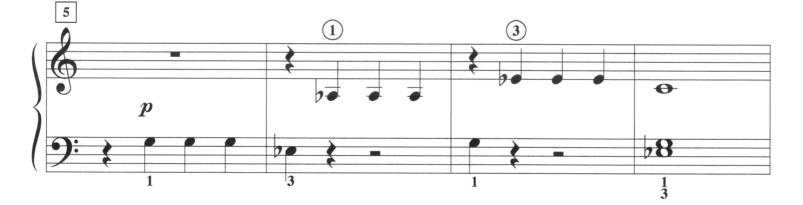

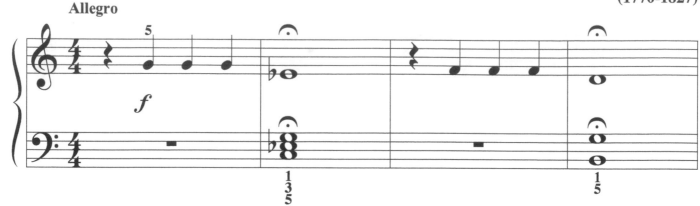

Teacher Duet: (Student plays 1 octave higher)

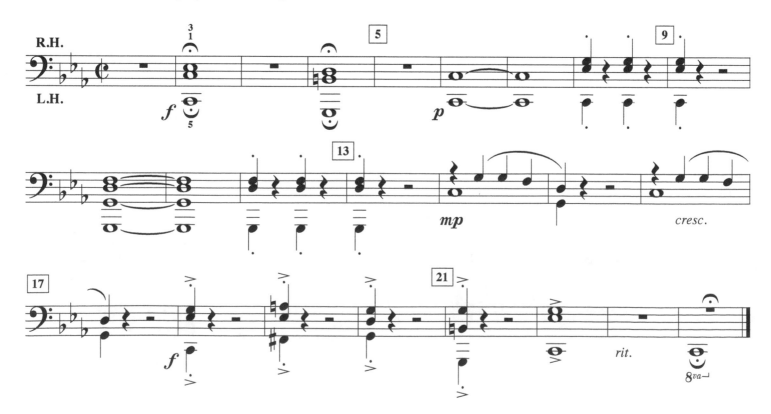

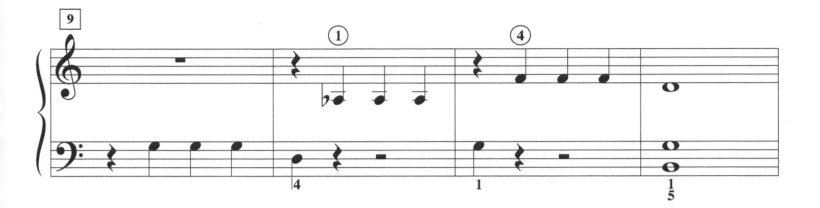

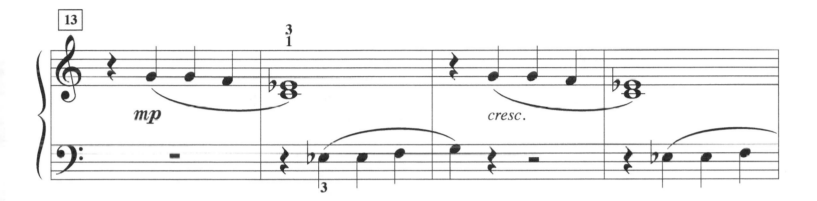

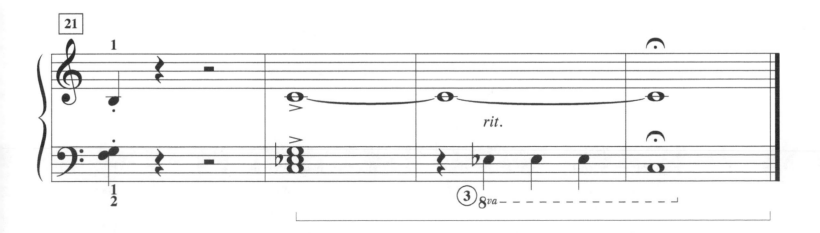

CLASSIC PIECES IN THE KEY OF C MAJOR
(with I, IV, and V7 Chords)

THEME FROM SYMPHONY NO. 6 ("Pastoral," Op. 68) - page 31
The "Pastoral" Symphony, Beethoven's sixth, has five movements. Beethoven gave each movement a title, although the music itself does not tell a story. Instead, the music depicts the changes and moods in nature. A violent thunderstorm erupts in the fourth movement. This gentle tune follows in the final movement, titled "Shepherd's Song: Happy, Thankful Feelings After the Storm."

SPRING, first movement (from *The Four Seasons*) - page 32
Vivaldi's music is dramatic, full of rhythmic and dynamic contrasts. Some of the composer's contemporaries thought his music was "bizarre." Vivaldi was an early champion of "program music," music which tells a story. *Spring* is the first of *The Four Seasons* string concertos. Its three movements capture the essence of that season – bird song, gentle breezes, passing storms, and new life.

THEME FROM *FINLANDIA* - page 34
Sibelius, the most famous of Finnish composers, wrote especially powerful works for symphony orchestra. With *Finlandia*, Sibelius presented a tribute to the Finnish people. Though it was not intended as such, it became a rallying cry for national independence. The Russian Czarist government actually banned performances of the piece during times of political unrest. *Finlandia* catapulted Sibelius to international fame.

PRINCE OF DENMARK'S MARCH - page 36
Jeremiah Clarke was organist and choirmaster at St. Paul's Cathedral in London. After Henry Purcell, he was the most famous English composer of his time. The "Prince of Denmark's March" is now often played at weddings and as a trumpet voluntary (a piece composed for a church service), but it was originally included in Clarke's *A Choice Collection of Ayres for the Harpsichord*.

MINUET (Op. 14, No. 1) - page 38
Paderewski was one of the most lionized concert pianists in the first half of the 20th century. As a fervent Polish patriot, he interrupted his concert career to serve for short periods as Prime Minister of the Polish Republic and as a delegate to the League of Nations. Although he wrote music in many forms, it was his piano music that attracted lasting attention. In fact, this minuet was played by almost every advancing piano student in the mid 1900s.

THEME FROM THE "SURPRISE" SYMPHONY - page 40
Haydn's Symphony No. 94 was one of the London Symphonies and, like several others in this group, it acquired a nickname – the "Surprise" Symphony. The second movement opens with quiet and refined string music. Then – surprise – there is a sudden explosion of sound. The whole orchestra comes in with a loud chord. In case any in the audience had fallen asleep, this would certainly wake them up!

CARO NOME (Theme from *Rigoletto*) - page 42

Although Verdi wrote other vocal and choral works (notably the *Requiem*), it is the 26 operas that assured his lasting fame. This aria from *Rigoletto* is sung in the first act by Gilda, the young daughter of the Rigoletto, who is the hunchback jester to the Duke of Mantua. When the womanizing Duke visits Gilda, he pretends to be a student and uses a false name. After he leaves, the smitten Gilda repeats his "dear name" *(caro nome)*.

RONDEAU (from *Suite de Symphonies,* No. 1) - page 44

Mouret's career centered in Paris. He directed the Paris Opera orchestra from 1714 to 1718 and, thereafter, served as composer/director of the French Theatre and the New Italian Theatre. His diverse catalog of works contains lyric comedies and opera-ballets, motets and cantatas, as well as *Suites de Symphonies* – sets of instrumental dances for small ensembles. This "Rondeau" is from the first suite. You probably know it as the theme music for *Masterpiece Theatre.*

THE TROUT (*Die Forelle*) - page 46

The *lieder* (art songs) that Schubert wrote are intensely expressive. In this song, *Die Forella* (The Trout), you can hear the swirling waters of the little brook in the piano accompaniment. Schubert again used this melody as the theme for a set of variations in his chamber music masterpiece, the "Trout" Quintet, a work scored for violin, viola, cello, double bass, and piano.

SPRING SONG (*Songs Without Words,* Op. 62, No. 6) - page 48

Felix Mendelssohn wrote music in almost every genre, popularized works of earlier composers such as Bach and Handel, founded the Leipzig Conservatory, and was a busy conductor. His many "Songs Without Words" (he wrote 52 throughout his lifetime) exemplify the 19th century interest in short, poetic solo piano works. The six piano pieces of Opus 62 were dedicated to Robert Schumann's wife Clara.

VARIATIONS ON A THEME BY HAYDN (St. Anthony's Chorale) - page 50

Brahms titled this work "Variations on a Theme by Haydn" because it is based on a theme *(Chorale St. Antoni)* from a work thought to be composed by Haydn. Brahms first wrote these variations for two pianos, and that version is still often performed. After sharing the piece with pianist Clara Schumann, Brahms orchestrated the work. Its success and popularity marked a turning point in Brahms' career and encouraged him to complete his first symphony. (See pages 4 and 14, Finale from Symphony No. 1.)

ARIA (Theme from *La Traviata*) - page 52

In his operas, Giuseppe Verdi combined the qualities of nationalism and universality in a way that was both dramatic and natural. The plot of *La Traviata* (The Wayward Woman) is based on Alexandre Dumas' novel *La Dame aux Camélias.* At a party in the opening act, the courtesan Violetta is introduced to Alfredo, who had longed to meet her and has fallen in love. They toast one another in this spirited drinking song.

KEY OF C

C Major Scale

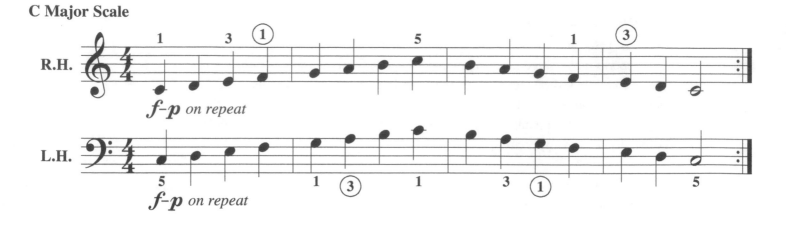

R.H.   *f-p* on repeat

L.H.   *f-p* on repeat

Primary Chords

The **I**, **IV**, and **V** chords are called the *primary* chords.

They are built on scale degrees 1, 4, and 5 of the major scale.

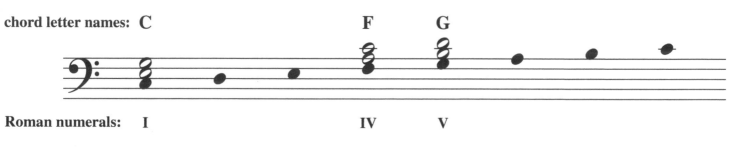

chord letter names: **C**   **F**   **G**

Roman numerals: **I**   **IV**   **V**

C, **F**, and **G** are the **I**, **IV**, and **V** chords in the Key of C.

Common Chord Positions

The chords above are shown in the *root position*, built up in 3rds from the chord *root* (chord name).

By inverting the notes, the **I**, **IV**, and **V7** chords can be played with little motion of the hand.

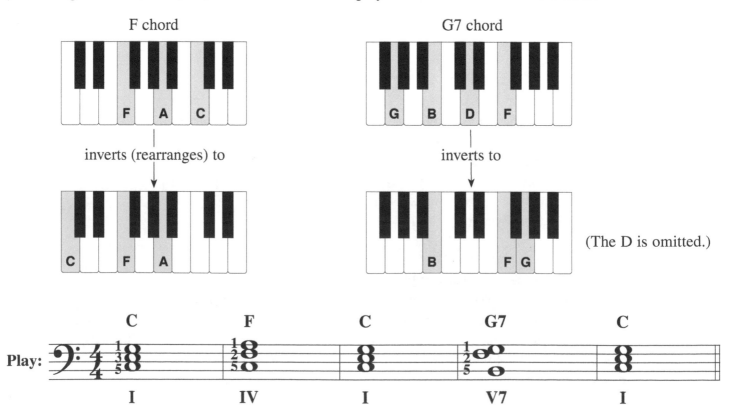

F chord   G7 chord

inverts (rearranges) to   inverts to

(The D is omitted.)

Play: C   F   C   G7   C

        I   IV   I   V7   I

Theme from
Symphony No. 6
("Pastoral," Op. 68)

Ludwig van Beethoven
(1770-1827)

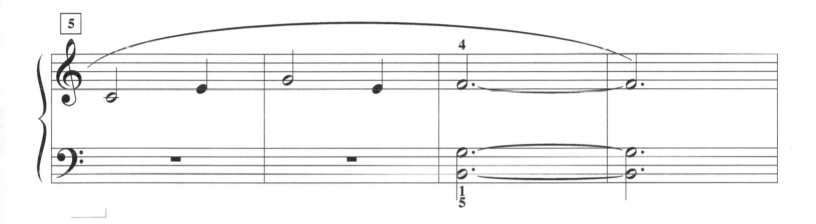

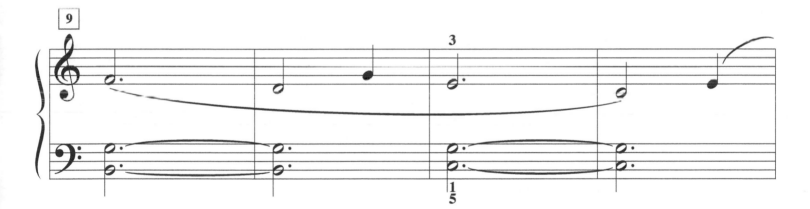

FF3030

Spring, 1st movement

(from *The Four Seasons*)

Antonio Vivaldi
(1678-1741)

Allegro (fast, cheerful)

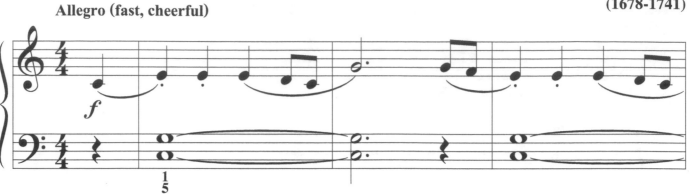

Teacher Duet: (Student plays 1 octave higher)

33

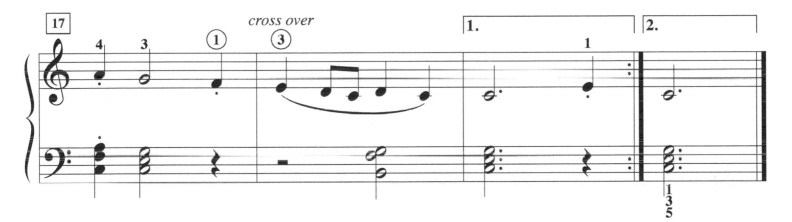

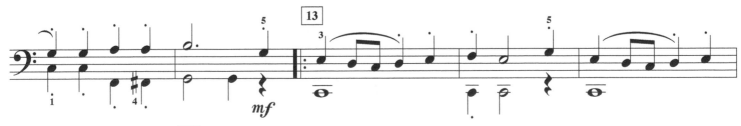

FF3030

Theme from Finlandia

Jean Sibelius
(1865-1957)

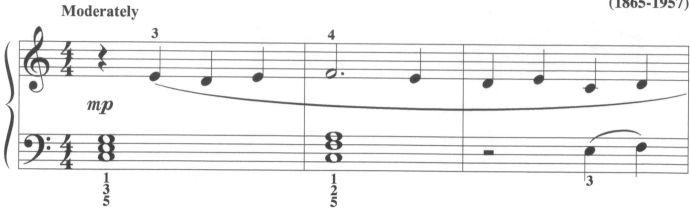

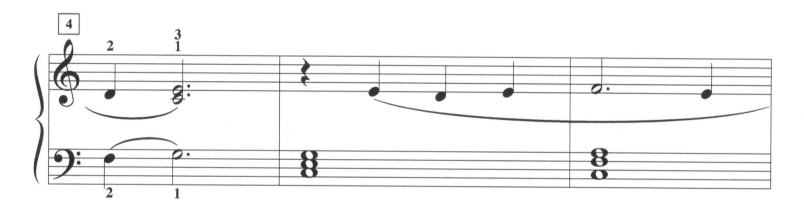

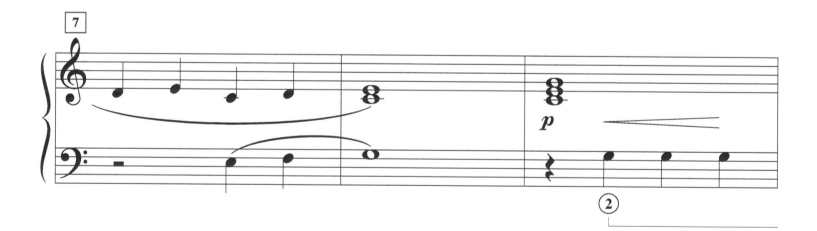

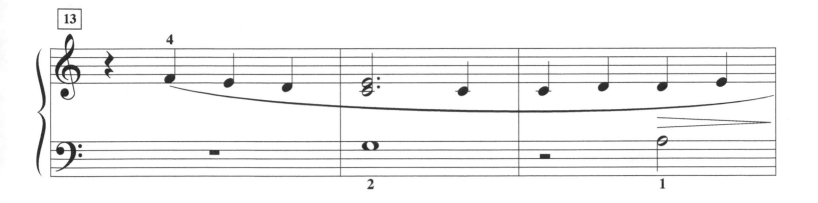

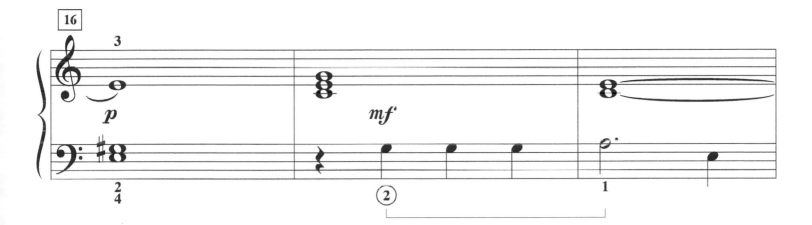

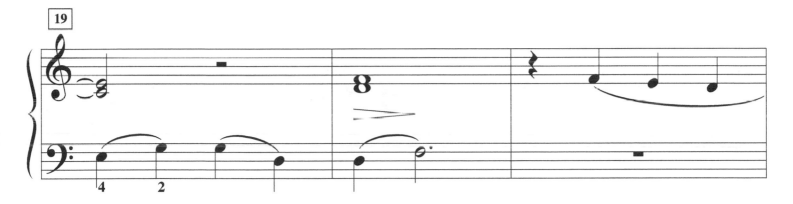

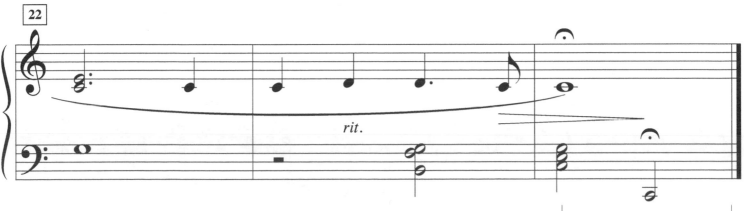

Prince of Denmark's March
(Trumpet Voluntary)

Jeremiah Clarke
(1674-1707)

Moderate March tempo

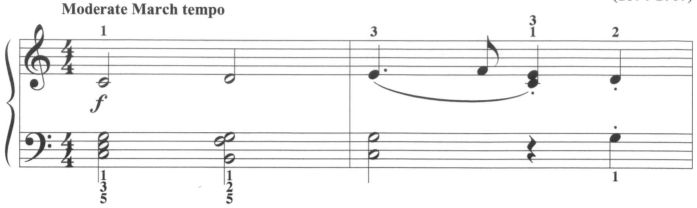

Teacher Duet: (Student plays 1 octave higher)

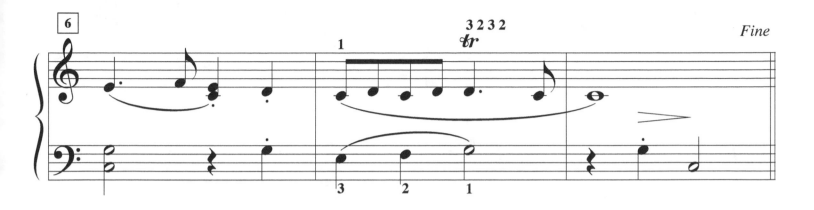

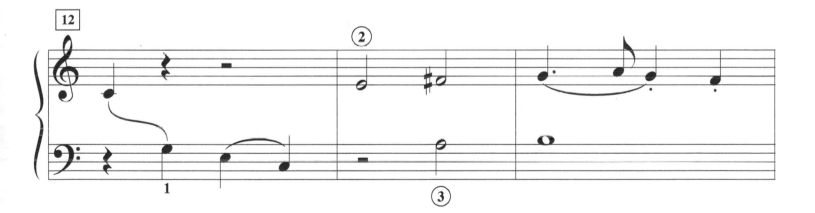

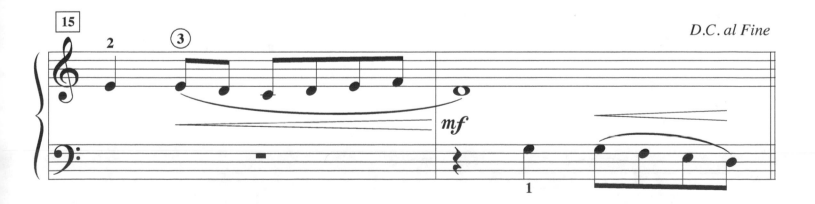

Minuet
(Op. 14, No. 1)

Ignacy Paderewski
(1860-1941)

Allegretto (cheerfully)

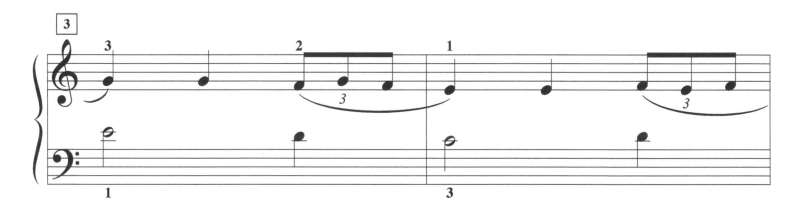

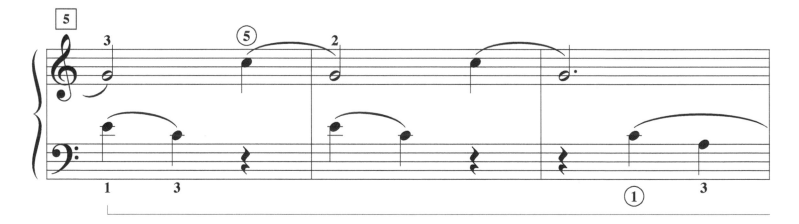

Teacher Duet: (Student plays 1 octave higher, and teacher pedals for duet)

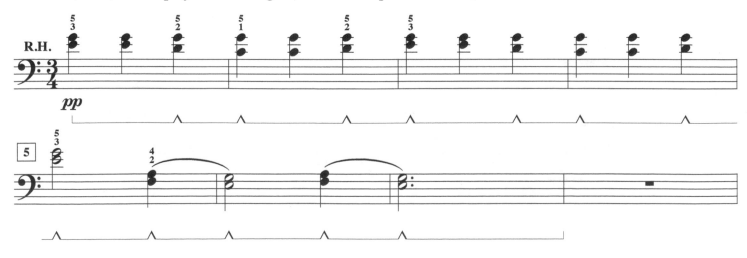

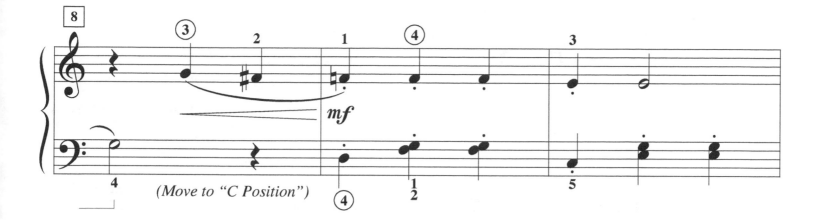

(Move to "C Position")

optional pedal

poco rit.

poco rit.

Theme from
The "Surprise" Symphony

Franz Joseph Haydn
(1732-1809)

Teacher Duet: (Student plays 1 octave higher)

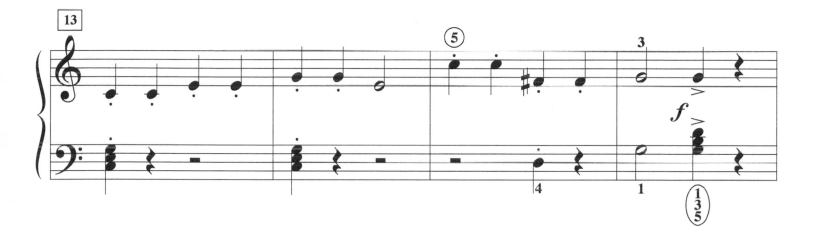

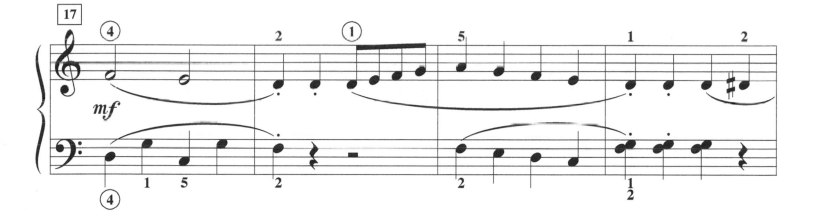

Teacher Note: The ♫ rhythm
may be taught by imitation.

Caro Nome
(Theme from *Rigoletto*)

Giuseppe Verdi
(1813-1901)

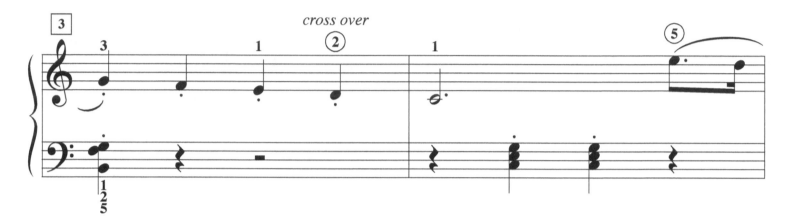

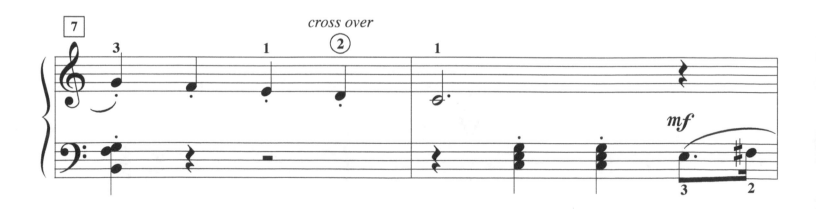

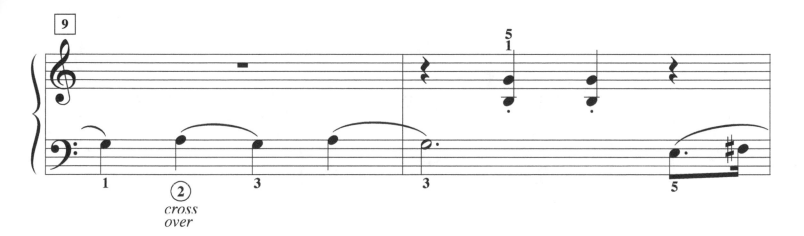

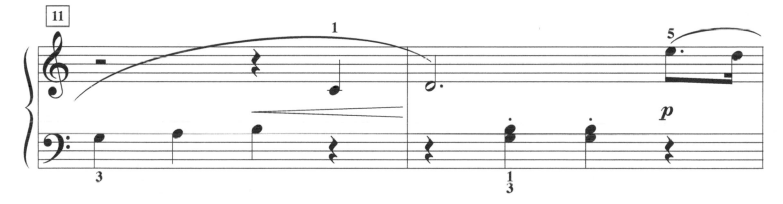

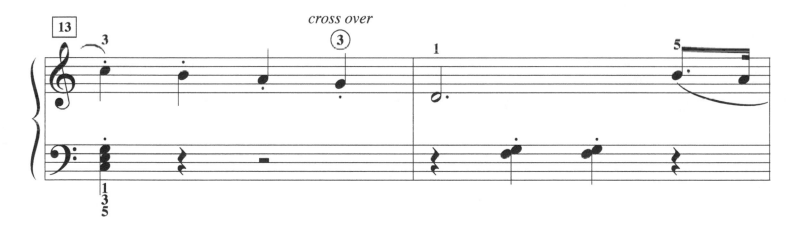

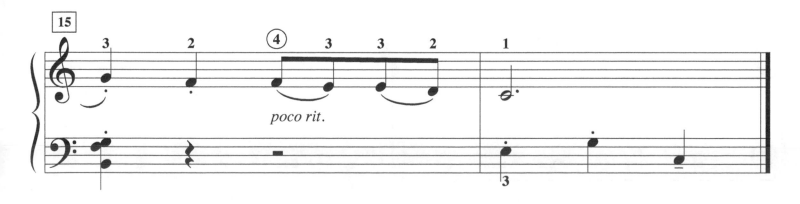

Rondeau

(from *Suite de Symphonies*, No. 1)

Jean-Joseph Mouret
(1682-1738)

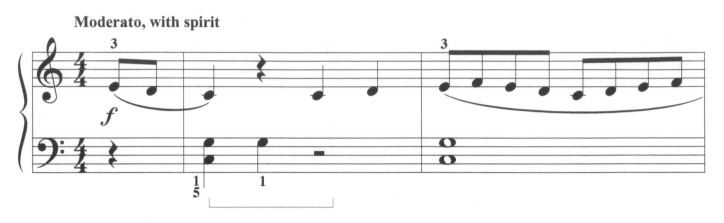

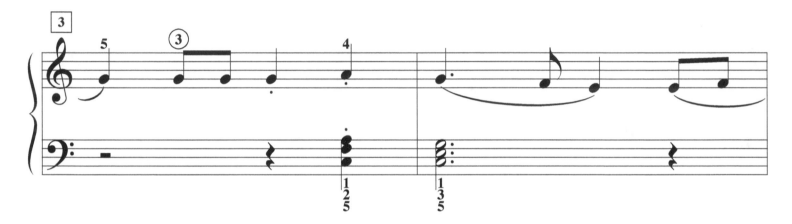

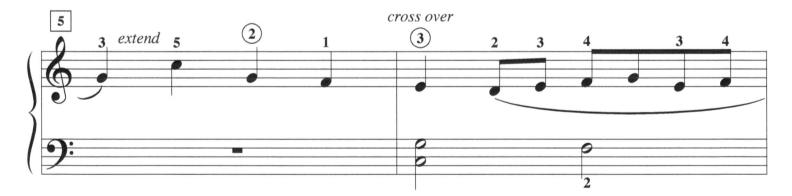

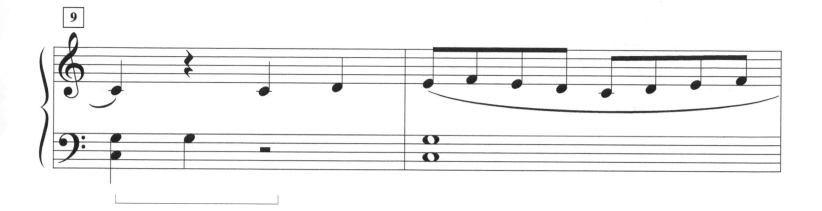

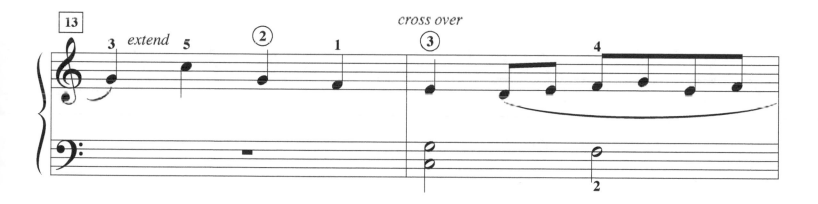

The Trout
(Die Forelle)

Franz Schubert
(1797-1828)

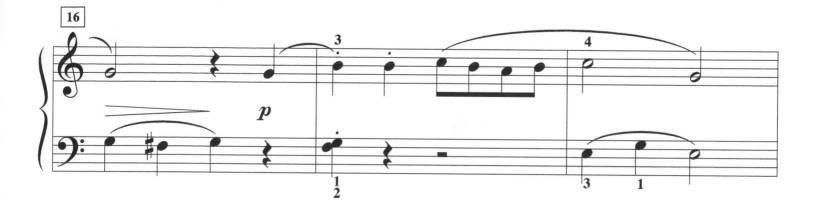

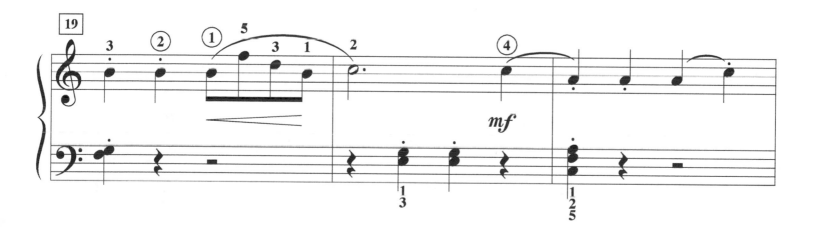

Spring Song
(from *Songs Without Words*, Op. 62, No. 6)

Felix Mendelssohn
(1809-1847)

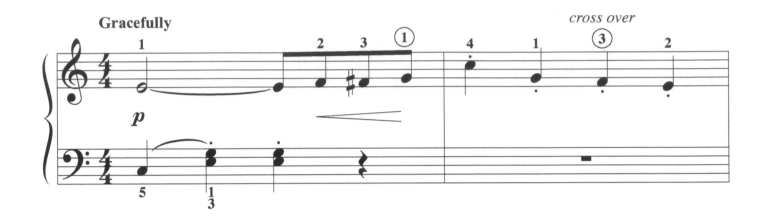

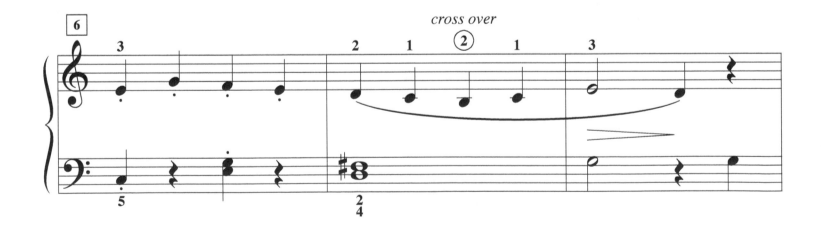

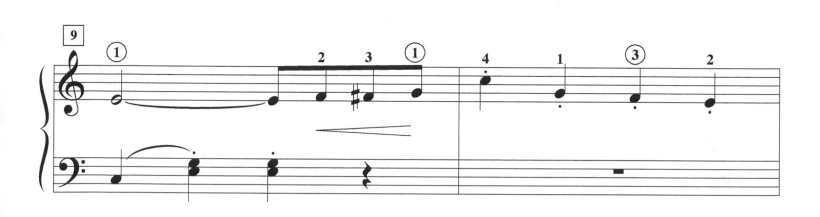

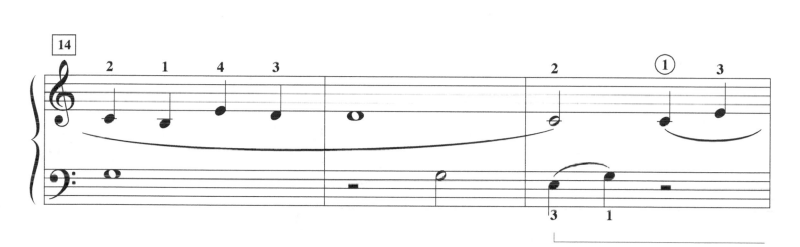

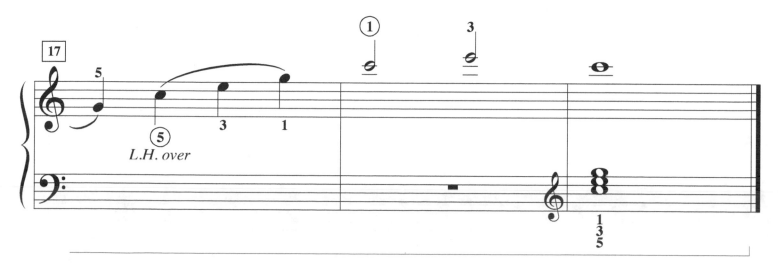

Variations on a Theme by Haydn

(St. Anthony's Chorale)

Johannes Brahms
(1833-1897)

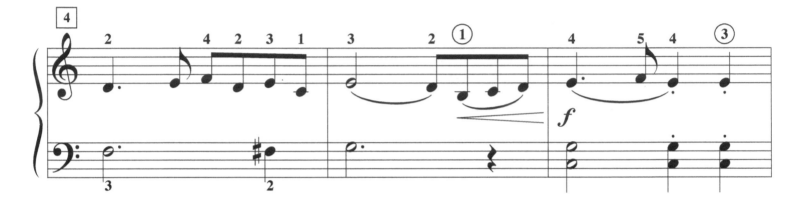

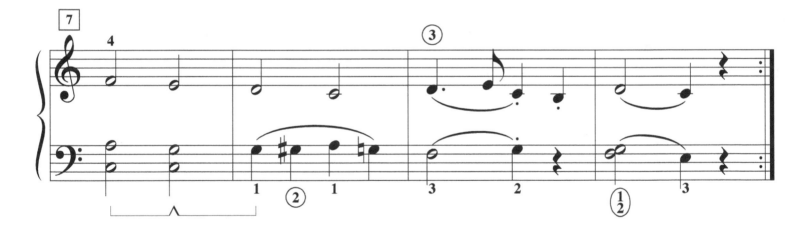

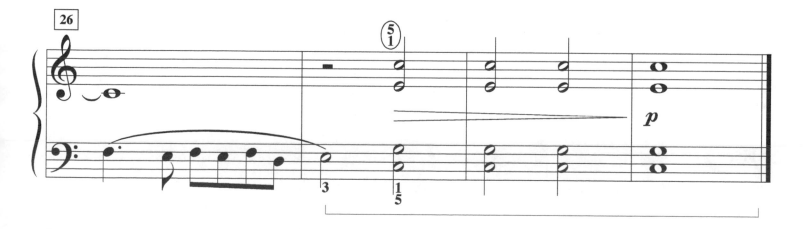

Aria
(Theme from *La Traviata*)

Giuseppe Verdi
(1813-1901)

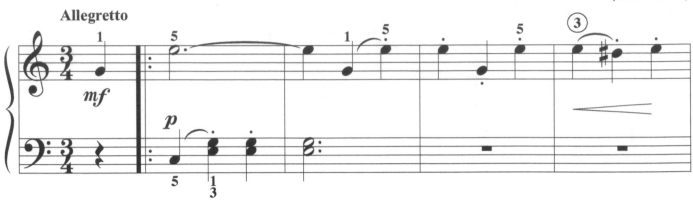

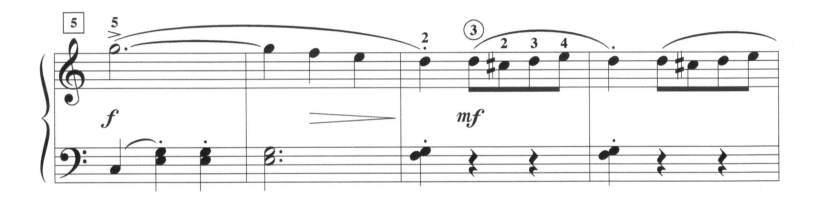

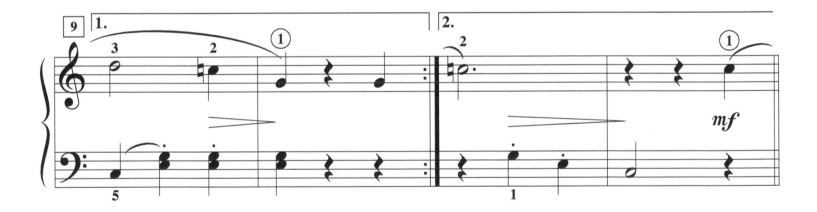

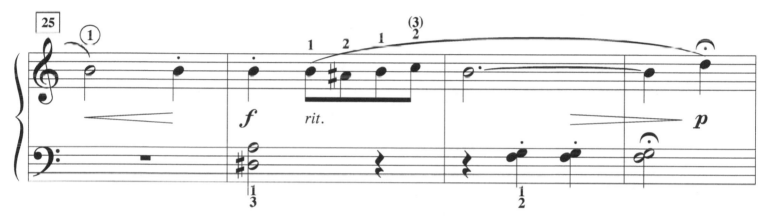

CLASSIC PIECES
IN THE KEY OF G MAJOR
(with I, IV, and V7 Chords)

THEME (from Sonata in A Major, K. 331) - page 57

This lullaby-like music is the theme of a set of variations that opens Mozart's *Sonata in A Major*, K. 331. Beginning a sonata with a theme and variations was a departure from the expected norms. The theme may have been taken from a German folk song, but the careful way in which Mozart inserted slurs gives this otherwise rustic tune elegance and charm.

MARCH OF THE ENGLISH GUARD - page 58

In addition to his duties as organist at St. Paul's Cathedral, Jeremiah Clarke was also "Composer of the Musick used in the Theatre Royal (Drury Lane)." This march may have been written for trumpet and wind ensemble, or as a harpsichord piece in imitation of the trumpet style. It is certainly easy to hear it as a very proper march for trumpet and drums.

THEME FROM *THE MAGIC FLUTE* - page 60

This folk-like melody occurs in the finale to Act 1 of Mozart's opera The Magic Flute. Papageno, a bird-catcher, has been given a set of magic silver bells by three ladies who serve the Queen of the Night. Tamino, the hero-prince, has been given a magic flute. Playing on these instruments, Papageno and Tamino overcome all the trials and difficulties associated with rescuing the Princess.

LAUGHING SONG (from *Die Fledermaus*) - page 62

The plot of Johann Strauss' best-known operetta ("The Bat") involves a series of farcical mix-ups. In Act Two, Adele, chambermaid to the wealthy Rosalinde, comes to the costume ball disguised in her mistress's clothes. Rosalinde's husband is attracted to Adele, but mentions that she reminds him of his wife's maid. In her "Laughing Song," Adele jokes that he is not a good judge. How could a maid afford these clothes...have hands so soft...and feet so dainty?

AUTUMN, 3rd movement (from *The Four Seasons*) - page 64

During his lifetime, Vivaldi was better known as a violinist than a composer. After his death in 1741, his music was forgotten. Nearly a century later, when Felix Mendelssohn "rediscovere" the music of Bach, Vivaldi's music was brought to light, too, because Bach had transcribed some of Vivaldi's works. Chief among the works restored to prominence was Vivaldi's *The Four Seasons*.

SEE, THE CONQUERING HERO COMES (from the oratorio *Joshua*) - page 66

Handel was the foremost composer of Baroque operas and oratorios. This chorus, originally from the oratorio *Joshua*, was inserted by Handel into his later and more popular work *Judas Maccabeus*. Oratorios are usually based on religious texts and staged with soloists, chorus, and orchestra. Judas Maccabeus led the revolt against the Syrians who wished to impose their religion on the Jews. Maccabeus purified the Temple at Jerusalem, and event commemorated at Hanukkah.

THEME FROM *DON GIOVANNI* (*Là ci darem la mano*) - page 68

This music comes from *Don Giovanni* ("Don Juan"), one of Mozart's comic opera masterpieces. Don Juan – the scheming and lecherous gentleman of the title – and Zerlina, a peasant girl, sing a duet in which each tries to seduce the other. "Là ci darem la mano," sings the Don, "Come, give me your hand," Zerlina parries his invitation with coy remarks. In the end, it is Zerlina who makes the conquest!

LIEBESTRAUM (Dream of Love) - page 70

Franz Liszt was a spectacular pianist, and his concerts attracted frenzied audiences. But Liszt was also a prolific composer who wrote music for almost every medium. His piano music displays characteristics of his playing – rich sounds, sweeping flourishes, and changing colors. He wrote three *Liebesträume* (Dreams of Love), but it is the third in the set that has gained immortality.

FARANDOLE (from *L'Arlésienne*) - page 72

Bizet's music for *L'Arlésienne* ("The Woman from Arles") is a suite of orchestral pieces written to accompany the play by Alphonse Daudet. After Bizet's death, a friend used music from the original work to form a second orchestral suite. The "Farandole" is from this suite. A *farandole* is a line dance native to southern France in the region around Arles. The linked dancers follow a leader along a winding path.

BARCAROLLE (from *The Tales of Hoffmann*) - page 74

Offenbach's most succesful work, *Les contes d'Hoffmann* ("The Tales of Hoffmann"), was his attempt at writing grand opera, but many changes were made to the work after his death. The plot is based on the stories of E.T.A. Hoffmann in which he reminisces about his love life. The "Barcarolle" (boat song) is heard in Act Four as Giulietta, one of his lovers, arrives in a gondola on the Grand Canal in Venice.

O MIO BABBINO CARO (from *Gianni Schicchi*) - page 76

The plot of this short opera by Puccini is based on two characters named in Canto XXX of Dante's *Inferno*. Schicchi is a wily peasant who disguises himself as a dying man, at the request of the man's family, in order to change the already-dead man's will. Schicchi's own daughter loves a nephew in this family, so she, too, begs her father to play this trick. *O mio babbino caro* translates to "Oh, my dear father."

KEY OF G

G Major Scale

f-p on repeat

f-p on repeat

Primary Chords in G

REVIEW: The primary chords are built on scale degrees 1, 4, and 5 of the major scale.

NEW: Here are the **I**, **IV**, and **V** chords in the Key of G.

chord letter names: **G**   **C**   **D**

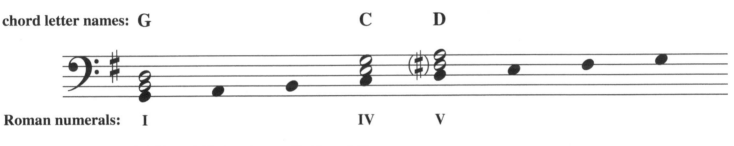

Roman numerals: **I**   **IV**   **V**

In the Key of G the **I**, **IV**, and **V** chords are **G**, **C**, and **D**.

Common Chord Positions

By inverting the notes, the **I**, **IV**, and **V7** chords can be played with little motion of the hand.

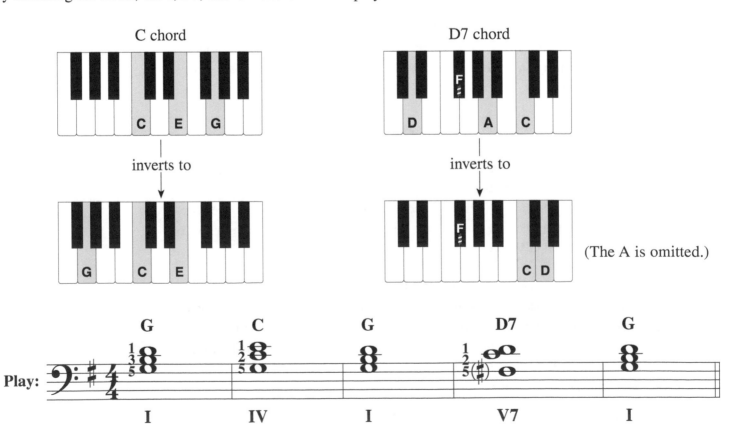

Theme from
Sonata in A Major
(K. 331)

Wolfgang Amadeus Mozart
(1756-1791)

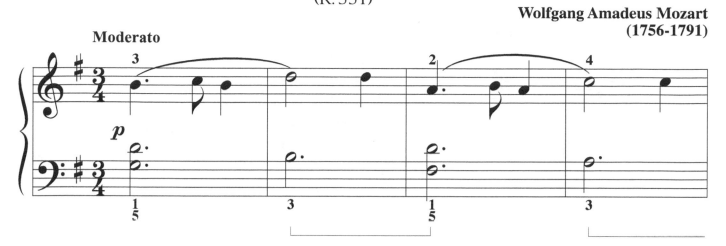

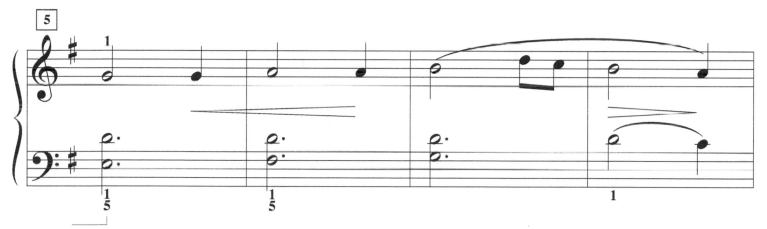

FF3030

March of the English Guard

Jeremiah Clarke
(1674-1707)

Moderate March tempo

Teacher Duet: (Student plays 1 octave higher)

Theme from
The Magic Flute

Wolfgang Amadeus Mozart
(1756-1791)

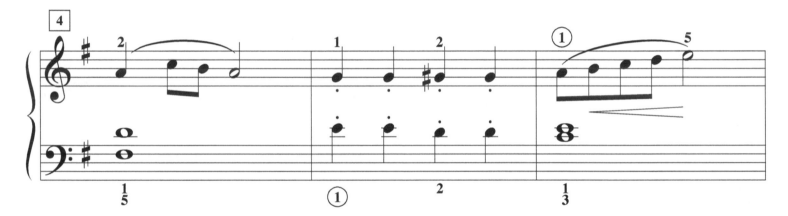

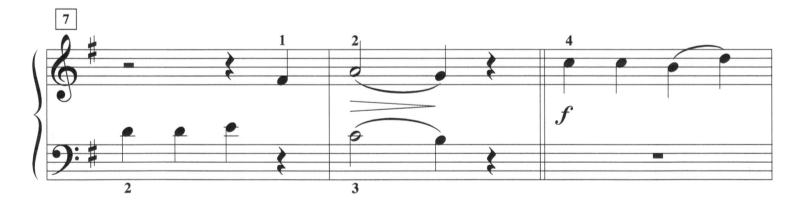

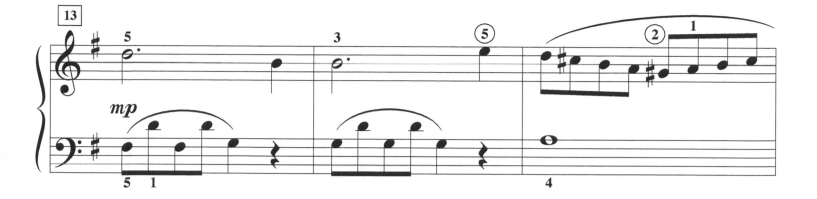

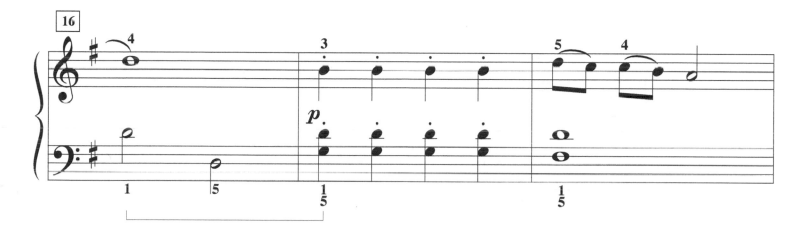

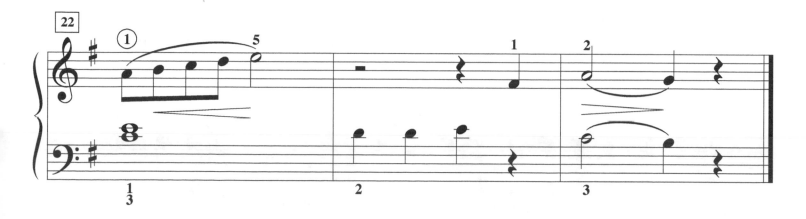

Laughing Song
(from the operetta *Die Fledermaus*)

Johann Strauss, Jr.
(1825-1899)

Teacher Duet: (Student plays 1 octave higher, teacher pedals for duet)

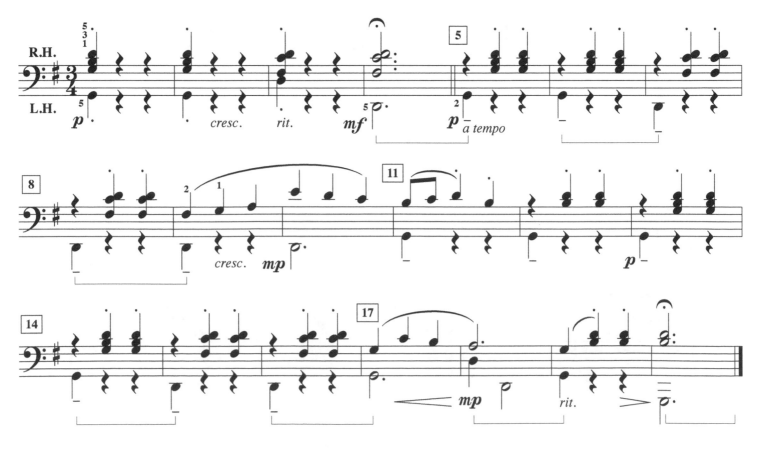

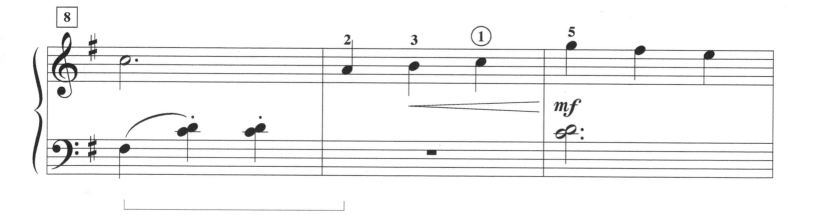

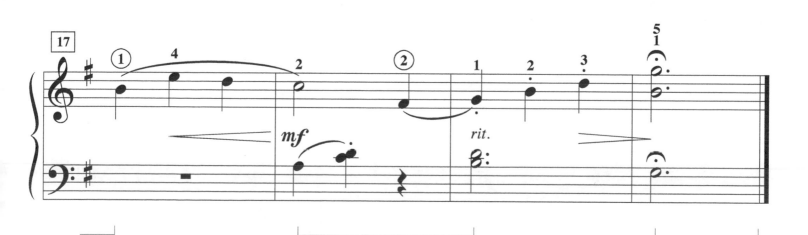

Autumn

3rd movement

(from *The Four Seasons*)

Antonio Vivaldi
(1678-1741)

See, the Conquering Hero Comes

(from the oratorio *Joshua*)

George Frideric Handel
(1685-1759)

Majestically

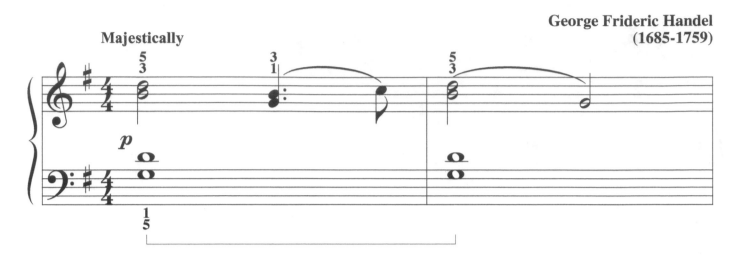

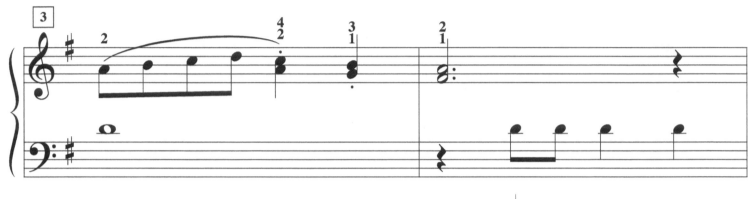

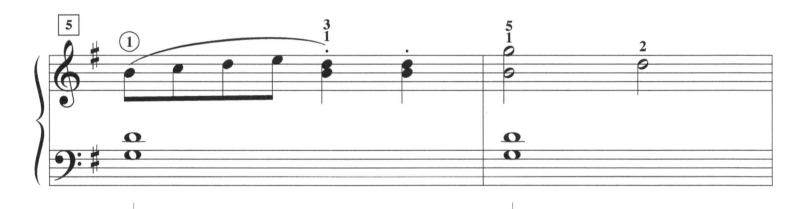

cross over

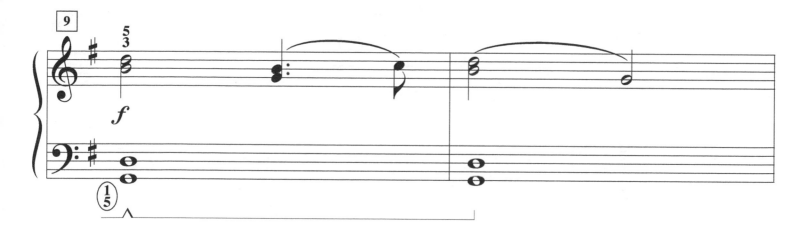

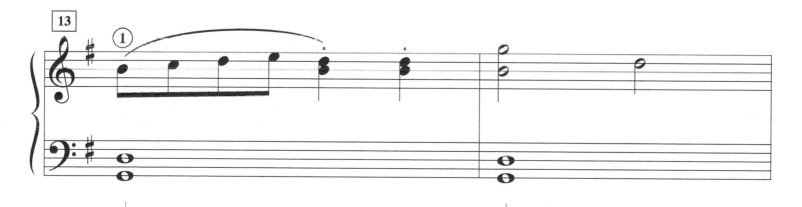

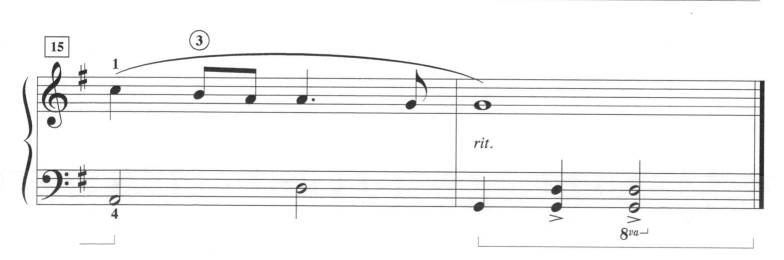

Theme from Don Giovanni
(Là ci darem la mano)

Wolfgang Amadeus Mozart
(1756-1791)

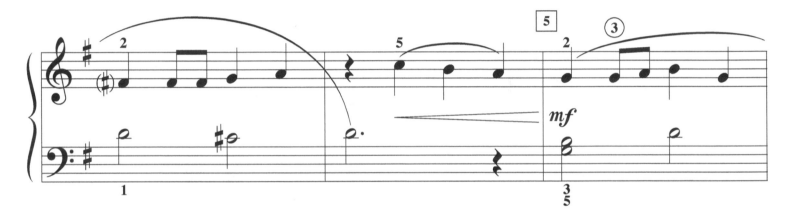

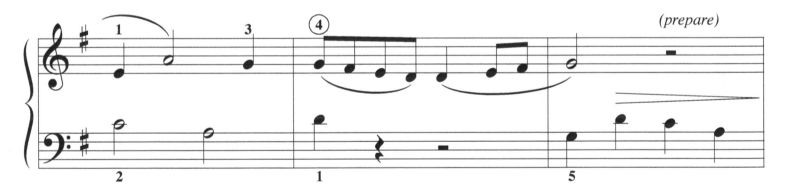

Teacher Duet: (Student plays 1 octave higher)

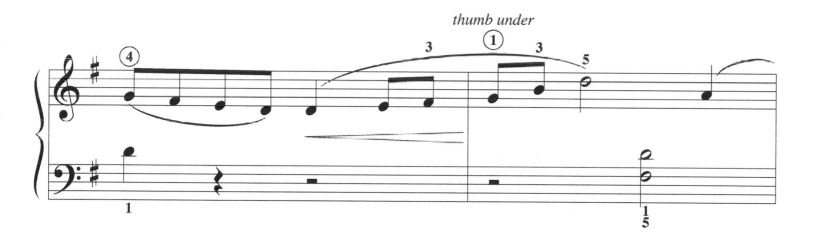

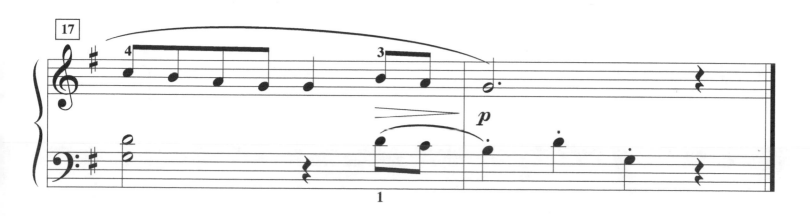

Liebestraum
(Dream of Love)

Franz Liszt
(1811-1886)

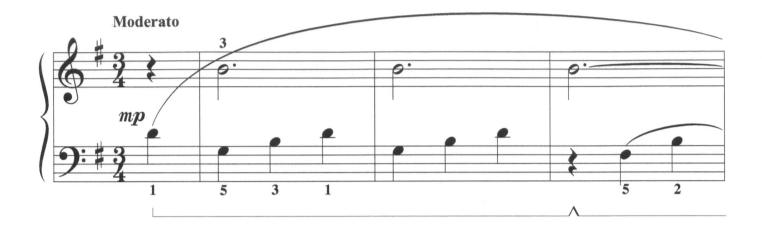

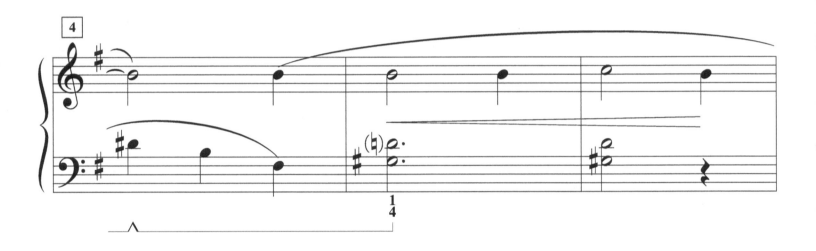

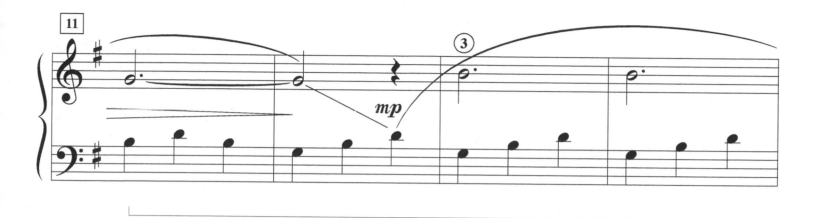

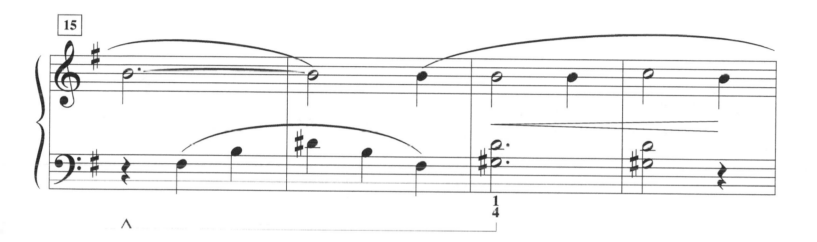

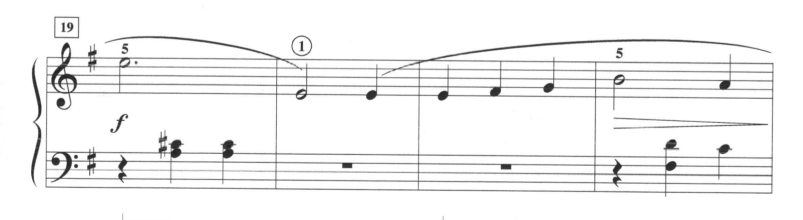

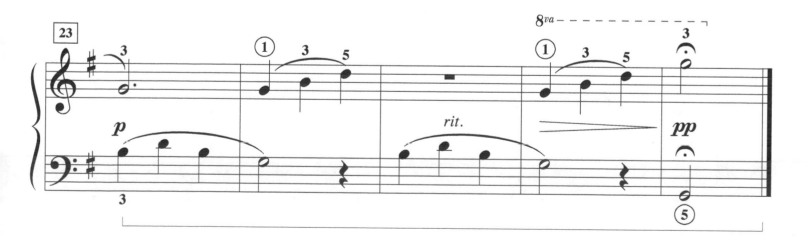

Farandole

(from *L'Arlésienne*)

Georges Bizet
(1838-1875)

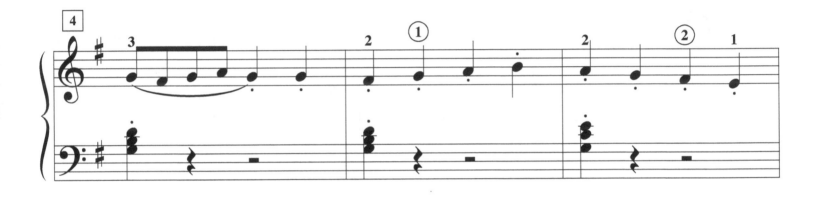

73

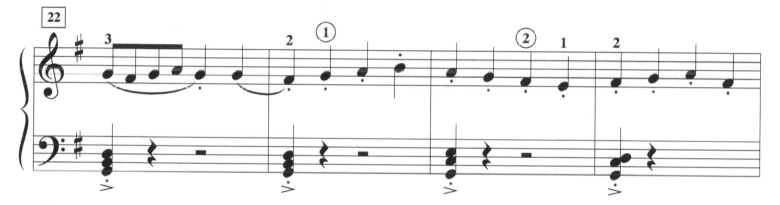

FF3030

Barcarolle

(from the opera *The Tales of Hoffmann*)

Jacques Offenbach
(1819-1880)

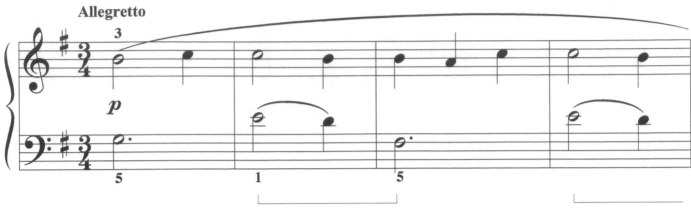

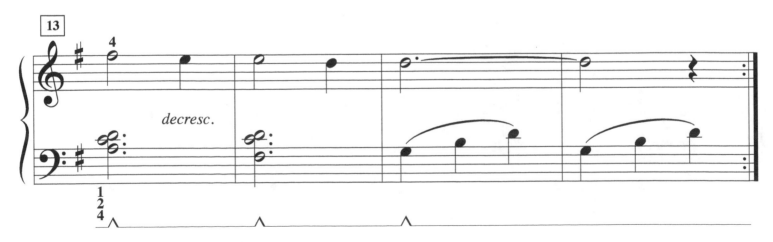

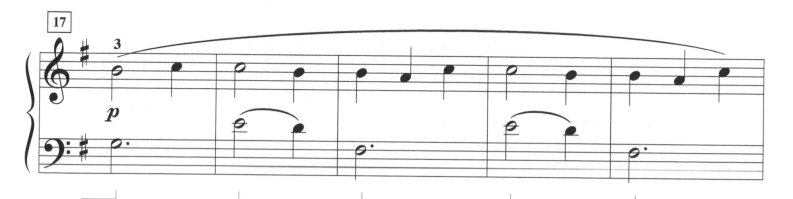

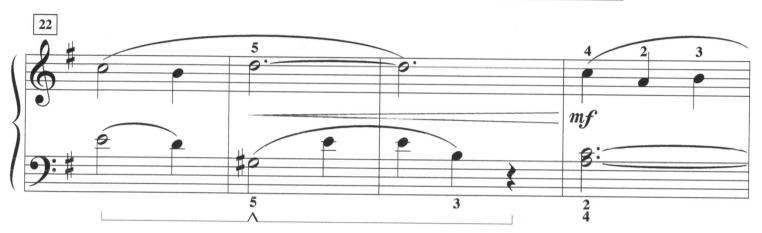

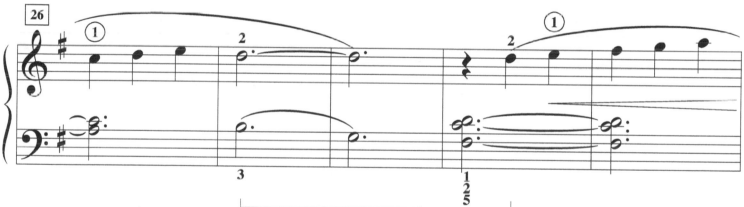

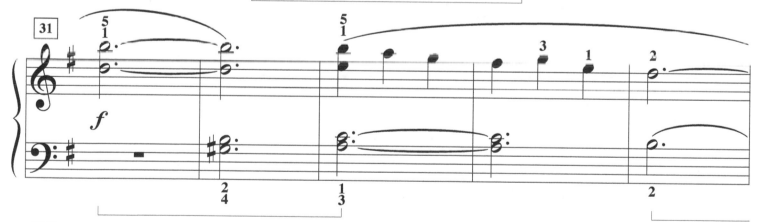

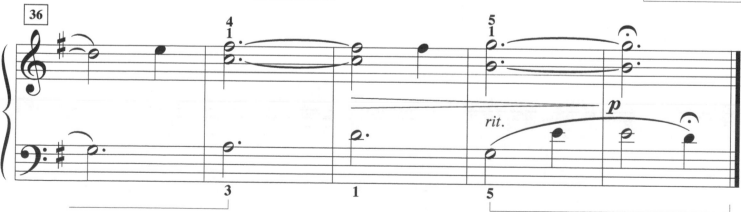

O mio babbino caro

(from *Gianni Schicchi*)

Giacomo Puccini
(1858-1924)

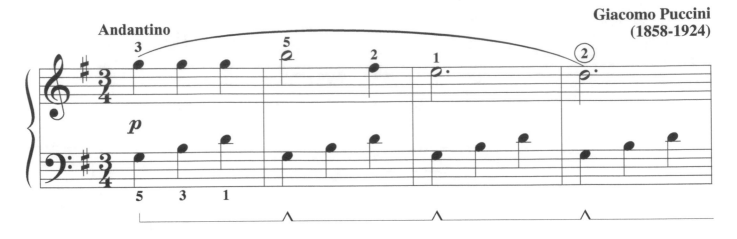

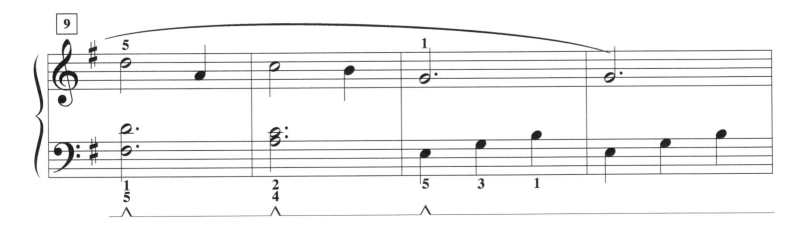

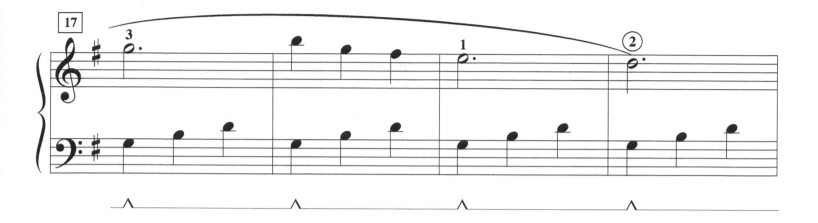

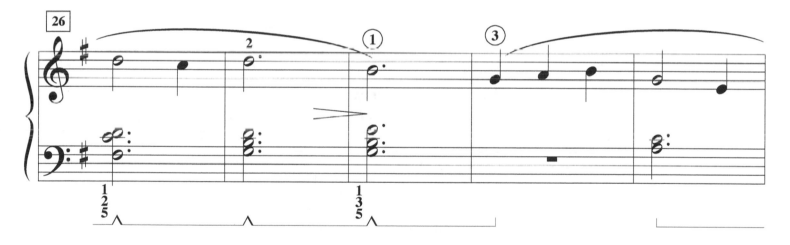

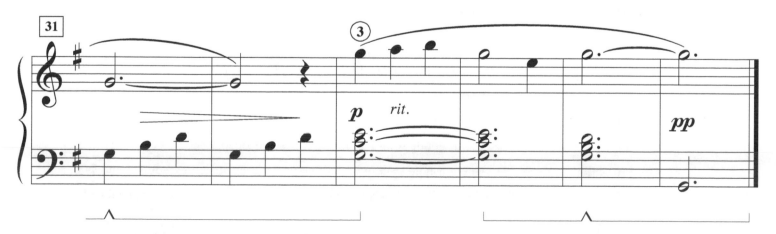

FF3030

DICTIONARY OF MUSICAL TERMS

DYNAMIC MARKS

pp	*p*	*mp*	*mf*	*f*
pianissimo	*piano*	*mezzo piano*	*mezzo forte*	*forte*
very soft	soft	moderately soft	moderately loud	loud

crescendo (cresc.)
Play gradually louder.

diminuendo (dim.) or decrescendo (decresc.)
Play gradually softer.

SIGN	TERM	DEFINITION
	accent mark	Play this note louder.
	accidentals	Sharps, flats, or naturals added to a piece and not in the key signature.
	aria	A song for one or two voices with an instrumental accompaniment, usually from an opera or cantata.
	barcarolle	A boat song characterized by a gentle rocking rhythm.
	ballet	Musical theater which uses dance to tell a story. Besides dance, ballet uses music, scenery, and costumes (but no singing).
	C major scale	An eight-note scale (C-D-E-F-G-A-B-C) with half steps between scale degrees 3-4 and 7-8.
	cantata	A vocal musical work based on a text, usually with several movements such as arias, duets, and choruses.
	concerto	A composition for a solo instrument and orchestra. A concerto spotlights the virtuoso (brilliant) playing of the soloist.
	damper pedal	The right pedal, which sustains the sound, played with the right foot.
	fermata	Hold this note longer than its normal value.
	finale	The last movement of a symphony, sonata, or act of an opera.
	1st and 2nd endings	Play the 1st ending and repeat from the beginning (or the facing repeat sign). Then play the 2nd ending, skipping over the 1st ending.
♭	**flat**	A flat lowers a note one half step.
	G major scale	An eight-note scale (G-A-B-C-D-E-F♯-G) with half steps between scale degrees 3-4 and 7-8.
	half step	The distance from one key to the very closest key on the keyboard. (Ex. C-C♯, or E-F).
	key signature	The key signature appears at the beginning of each line of music. It indicates sharps or flats to be used throughout the piece.
	ledger line	A short line used to extend the staff.
	legato	Smooth, connected.
	lullaby	A soft, gentle song for lulling a child to sleep.
	major scale	An eight-note scale with half steps between scale degrees 3-4 and 7-8.
	march	A piece of music used for marching, usually with two beats or four beats in a measure.
	minuet	An elegant dance in $\frac{3}{4}$ time. The dance was popular in the 1700s.

	Term	Definition
♮	**natural**	A natural (always a white key) cancels a sharp or a flat.
	octave	The interval which spans 8 letter names. (Ex. C to C)
	opera	A drama set to music, with singing, acting, and sometimes, dancing. In an opera, the characters express themselves by singing instead of speaking.
	operetta	A small opera, often a comedy. The musicals of today are modern operettas.
	opus	"Work." A composer's compositions are often cataloged in sequence, with each work given an *opus* number. Several pieces may be included in a single opus. Ex. Op. 3, No. 1; Op. 3, No. 2, etc.
	oratorio	A major composition based on a religious text which may include vocal solos, choruses, instrumental ensembles, and a narrator.
8*va*	***ottava***	Play one octave higher (or lower) than written.
	overture	An orchestral piece which begins an opera. The overture usually contains themes heard later in the opera.
	pedal mark	Shows the down-up motion of the damper pedal.
	phrase	A musical sentence. A phrase is often shown by a slur, also called a phrase mark.
	polka	A quick dance with a feel of two beats per measure.
‖: :‖	**repeat sign**	Play the music within the repeat signs again.
rit.	***ritardando***	Gradually slowing down.
	romance	A lyrical song for voice or lyric instrumental composition.
	rondeau	The French term for a rondo, a piece that has a recurring A section. Ex. A B A C A
	scale	From the Latin word *scala*, meaning "ladder." The notes of a scale move up or down by 2nds (steps).
♯	**sharp**	A sharp raises the note one half step.
	sixth (6th)	The interval that spans six letter names (Ex. E up to C, or A down to C). On the staff a 6th is written line-(skip 2 lines)-space or space-(skip 2 spaces)-line.
	slur	A curved line that indicates legato playing.
	sonata	An instrumental piece, often with 3 movements.
	staccato	Detached, disconnected.
	suite	A set of short pieces, often written in dance forms.
	symphony	A major composition for orchestra. A symphony has several sections called movements (ususally four).
	tempo	The speed of the music.
	tenuto mark	Stress the note by pressing gently into the key.
	theme	The main melody of a composition. (Many works have more than one theme.)
	tie	A curved line that connects two notes on the same line or space. Hold for the total counts of both notes.
¾ ⁴⁄₄	**time signature**	Two numbers at the beginning of a piece (one above the other). The top number indicates the number of beats per measure; the bottom number represents the note receiving the beat.
	triplet	3 eighth notes to a quarter note.
	upbeat (pick-up note)	The note(s) of an incomplete opening measure.
	voluntary	An organ piece, often with florid passages, used for a church service.
	waltz	A dance in ¾ time. Waltzes have continued to be popular from the 1800s to today.

COMPOSER INDEX